WITHDRAWN
UTSA LIBRARIES

why aren't we getting through?
THE URBAN COMMUNICATION CRISIS

why aren't we getting through?

THE URBAN COMMUNICATION CRISIS

Edited by EDMUND M. MIDURA

WILLIAM MONROE, JR.
WOLF VON ECKARDT
JAMES W. ROUSE
JOHN H. JOHNSON
BUDD SCHULBERG
JOSEPH W. SHOQUIST
PHILIP S. HEISLER
BRADLEY S. GREENBERG
BENJAMIN HOLMAN
ROYCE HANSON

 PUBLISHED BY **ACROPOLIS BOOKS LTD.** / WASHINGTON, D.C. 20009

This book is the result of the "Baltimore Sun Distinguished Lecture Series," a project of the Department of Journalism, University of Maryland. The lectures were made possible by a grant from the A. S. Abell Company Foundation and the Baltimore Sunpapers.

Special gratitude is due to Mr. William F. Schmick, Jr., President of the A. S. Abell Company Foundation; Mr. Perry J. Bolton, Assistant to the President of the Foundation; and Mr. Philip S. Heisler, Managing Editor of the Baltimore Evening Sun, who were instrumental in getting the Lecture Series started.

The purpose of the Lecture Series and its subsequent book publication is to provide a forum for the expression of ideas by distinguished journalists, scholars of journalism and others, and to provide a continuing medium of education and exchange between the Journalism Department, its students and alumni, and the journalism profession.

CONTEMPORARY ISSUES IN JOURNALISM
Volume I: Politics and the Press
Volume II: Why Aren't We Getting Through?

EDITORIAL BOARD
Ray Eldon Hiebert, Chairman

Lee M. Brown	Alfred A. Crowell
Carter R. Bryan	Philip C. Geraci
Charles C. Flippen II	Richard W. Lee
James E. Grunig	L. John Martin
Edmund M. Midura	D. Earl Newsom

Michael J. Petrick

© *Copyright 1971, Department of Journalism, University of Maryland*

All rights reserved. Except for the inclusion of brief quotations in a review, no part of this book may be reproduced or utilized in any form or by any means, electronic or mechanical, including photocopying, recording or by any information storage and retrieval system, without permission in writing from the publisher.

ACROPOLIS BOOKS
*Colortone Building, 2400 17th St., N.W.
Washington, D.C. 20009*

Printed in the United States of America by
COLORTONE PRESS, Creative Graphics Inc.
Washington, D.C. 20009

Type set in Times Roman and Futura Medium by Colortone Typographic Division, Inc.

Design by Design and Art Studio 2400, Inc.

Library of Congress Catalog Number 70-148676

Standard Book No. 87491-312-8 (cloth)
87491-316-0 (paper)

Contents

8 INTRODUCTION

13 MASS COMMUNICATION BEHAVIORS OF THE URBAN POOR
by Bradley S. Greenberg, Associate Professor of Communication, Michigan State University

29 HOW DOES A METROPOLITAN DAILY NEWSPAPER COVER THE INNER CITY?
by Philip S. Heisler, Managing Editor, The *Baltimore Evening Sun*

43 THE ROLE OF THE PRESS IN A CONTINUING URBAN CRISIS
by Joseph W. Shoquist, Managing Editor, The *Milwaukee Journal*

61 WHAT CAN BROADCASTERS DO TO BREAK THE INNER-CITY COMMUNICATION BARRIER?
by William Monroe, Jr., Washington Editor, NBC "Today" Program

87 WHAT CAN THE BLACK COMMUNICATOR DO TO BREAK THE INNER-CITY COMMUNICATION BARRIER?
by John H. Johnson, Publisher and Editor, *Ebony* Magazine

99 HOW CAN THE FEDERAL GOVERNMENT FACILITATE COMMUNICATION WITHIN THE CITY?
by Benjamin F. Holman, Director, Community Relations Service, U. S. Department of Justice

113 CAN THE DISADVANTAGED IN THE INNER CITY LEARN TO COMMUNICATE?
by Budd Schulberg, Author, Founder of Watts Writers Workshop

133 HOW CAN THE PEOPLE'S VOICE BE HEARD IN THE INNER CITY?
by Royce Hanson, President, Washington Center for Metropolitan Studies

151 THE FUTURE OF COMMUNICATION IN MEGALOPOLIS
by Wolf Von Eckardt, Architecture Critic, The *Washington Post*

167 URBAN COMMUNICATION: WHAT ARE THE "NEW CITIES" DOING?
by James W. Rouse, Developer of Columbia, Maryland

187 INDEX

★★★★★★★★★★★★★★★★★★★★★★★★

This is our basic conclusion: Our nation is moving toward two societies, one black, one white—separate and and unequal....

... the news media, ironically, have failed to communicate. They have not communicated to the majority of their audience ... a sense of the degradation, misery and hopelessness of living in the ghetto....

★★★★★★★★★★★★★★★★★★★★★★★★

. . . The alternative [to two societies] will require a commitment to national action—compassionate, massive, and sustained, backed by the resources of the most powerful and the richest nation on this earth. From every American it will require new attitudes, new understanding, and, above all, new will.

—The National Advisory Commission on Civil Disorders, 1968

All this will not be finished in the first 100 days, nor will it be finished in the first 1,000 days . . . nor perhaps in our lifetimes on this planet. But let us begin.

—John F. Kennedy, January 20, 1961

Introduction

The succession of "long, hot summers" that tortured such cities as Los Angeles, Detroit, Cleveland, Newark, Washington, Baltimore, Rochester, and Milwaukee during the 1960's finally made clear to Americans the fact that something was dreadfully wrong in their major urban centers. To be sure, problems had been apparent before then — the cities were physically decaying, population growth was stagnating or reversing, financing city government was becoming more and more difficult. But it took the riots and disorders to show that the social problem was far more serious than the physical or fiscal problems. The inner city was a time bomb, and it was ticking.

The inner city is a handy term to describe the urban concentrations of people, mostly black and Latin American, whose lot is deficient in almost every respect—jobs, housing, education, environment, cultural opportunities, health, *ad infinitum*. They are people pent up in hot, dirty, decaying cities with almost no hope of anything better. They are pent up because of all sorts of barriers—racial, physical, economic, cultural—and they are straining to break out of these barriers. Their frustration and alienation have inevitably resulted in urban disorders, which have made our cities—supposedly the crowning achievement of civilization—places to be feared, despised, and shunned.

INTRODUCTION

Not the least of the barriers that hem in the people of the inner city is what we have called here the communication barrier. Like the Berlin Wall, it is a barrier to those on both sides of it. The cement of our society is communication, and the mass communication system that we have developed is one of the finest and most pervasive in the world. Yet, for the people of the inner city, the benefits of this mass communication system are almost nonexistent. They have been unable to use it, except through the extreme tactic of civil disorder, to gain attention that might help to improve the misery of their lot. On the other hand, faced with this urban time bomb, the rest of society has been unable to reach the inner city through the mass media of communication with the messages and information that might forestall urban disorder and further worsening of the inner city's lot. That famed "two-way street" of communication has been blocked in both lanes.

The idea of this lecture series was to try to alleviate that situation by stimulating thought and discussion on how traffic on the two-way street might be stimulated. We knew that we would not solve the problem. It is too vast. But we felt that the light and heat generated by our group of eleven distinguished lecturers would help.

Our lecturers spoke in assigned areas in an attempt to take a comprehensive look at the whole question of the crisis in urban communication. Bradley S. Greenberg helped to set the stage by speaking on the mass communication behaviors of the urban poor, providing the necessary background with which to understand the problem of reaching people in the inner city. Philip S. Heisler, Joseph W. Shoquist, William Monroe, Jr., and John H. Johnson approached the problem from the point of view of the mass media, speaking on the problems of trying to reach the inner city and of the efforts being made by the media. Mr. Johnson had a double role in that he tried to explain the problems of a black communicator.

Discussing what could be done by government were Benjamin F. Holman and "Woody" Klein, who spoke from their experiences as federal and municipal officials. Mr. Klein, first press secretary to Mayor John V. Lindsay of New York, spoke on "How Can City Government Communicate?" but, unfortunately, his lecture could not be included in this book.

Mr. Klein's lecture was intended to complement Mr. Holman's talk on how the federal government can facilitate communication in the city. Having headed the public communication program of the nation's largest and most problem-ridden city, Mr. Klein was in a position to observe the problems of a municipal government trying to put the two-way street concept of communication into action with its citizens.

Mr. Klein told his audience that how a city communicates is becoming increasingly important because of the increasing necessity for public officials to try to enlist the aid of all city dwellers in the battle to save the cities. The streamlining of the city's communication apparatus—to try to get across Mayor Lindsay's program to New Yorkers in order to gain their support—became one of the first tasks of the incoming administration, Mr. Klein said.

Starting with the belief that they had a good program with which to deal with the city's problems, the Lindsay administration embarked upon communicating that program to citizens. Mr. Klein listed an eight-point communication program that was used in this effort: 1. The Mayor himself, speaking through his press conferences, background sessions with the press, statements by aides, public speeches, walks through the city, and his weekly television program; 2. the city commissioners, speaking as the experts in their particular areas; 3. a series of neighborhood "local city halls" at which the Mayor's aides were present to hear the complaints and suggestions of individual citizens; 4. a "mayor's information center," staffed by volunteers day and night to respond to telephone inquiries; 5. a "night-owl mayor" program in which top city officials stayed at City Hall overnight so that there was always someone on duty in case of emergencies (this activity received heavy coverage by the press for a time after it was started); 6. a professional staff to answer the thousands of letters received by the Mayor weekly; 7. the opening of offices in Albany and Washington to lobby for New York City's interests among the state and federal legislators; 8. a willingness for the Mayor or top aides to meet with special interest groups — ethnic, religious, economic — within the city to try to cope with pressing problems or to forestall impending crises. A constant emphasis upon repetition of the basics of the Lindsay administration program characterized the communication program and, Mr. Klein reported, it brought mixed results, depending upon how well the administration could articulate its point of view.

Examining, in the lecture series, what individuals from the inner city might themselves do were Royce Hanson and Budd Schulberg, the former from the point of view of political action and the latter from the point of view of educational action. Finally, taking imaginative looks at the future prospects and possibilities were Wolf Von Eckardt and James W. Rouse. Mr. Von Eckardt explored the "big picture" topic of community and Mr. Rouse explained one of the current efforts to re-establish community.

In all, they have presented us with much interesting, exciting—and even sobering—food for thought.

The editor, as chairman of the 1970 Distinguished Lectures Committee, is grateful for the assistance of Ray Eldon Hiebert and Richard W. Lee, both committee members, and especially grateful for that of my wife, Pam Mulhall Midura.

EDMUND M. MIDURA

College Park
July 1970

CHAPTER ONE

Mass Communication Behaviors of the Urban Poor

by
Bradley S. Greenberg
Associate Professor of Communication
Michigan State University

DR. GREENBERG has been one of our leading researchers in the area of communication and the poor, having participated in an impressive list of studies. In this role he has served as a consultant to the President's Commission on the Causes and Prevention of Violence and in many other consultative roles. He has written widely in the field of communication theory and communication effects. He is co-author of *The Kennedy Assassination and the American Public.* In addition to teaching communication subjects at Michigan State University, he has also taught at two other respected institutions, Stanford University and the University of Wisconsin. The material for his presentation in the Distinguished Lectures Series was drawn from his own research into communication behaviors of the urban poor in several different cities, and was subsequently presented in book form as *Use of the Mass Media by the Urban Poor* (1970).

THE 1960's ARE BEING DESCRIBED as the decade of work in the areas of poverty and race. Vast educational and welfare programs were and are still being directed at the poor. Yet the program sponsors have found that they had little basis for understanding how best to obtain awareness for their programs, let alone acceptance of those programs. Almost no empirical data were available on the communication behaviors of the poor, or on how to reach them. For example, the Kerner Commission was able to cite but one study in its report as background for describing the mass media behavior of ghetto residents. It is in this context that we have been examining communication behavior among the urban poor for the last three years.

In that time, we have directed four studies—in Lansing, Philadelphia, East Cleveland, and Cleveland. In them, we obtained data from parallel samples of low-income people of the general population. Our samples of low-income persons included equivalent groups of low-income whites and low-income blacks. In Lansing, we dealt with adults, in Philadelphia, with teenagers, and in East Cleveland, with pre-teens.

What I propose to do here is to develop a panoramic view of the use and functions of mass communications for urban poor people as they progress from childhood through adolescence to adult status. I recognize that data gathered at a single point in time from three age groups does not permit me to talk about developmental phenomena, only about age or generational differences. Yet it is the great similarity of communications behaviors that we found for each of these age groups that is quite striking.

In this research, we focused on four major aspects of mass communication behavior: ownership or access to the mass media, use of the mass media, attitudes toward the mass media and functions of the mass media. Let us begin this trek then in East Cleveland with an examination of the mass communication behaviors of some four hundred 4th and 5th graders.

As might be imagined, at this age level, the predominant mass medium is television. For our children from poor families, ownership is no problem whatsoever; on the average they had two working television sets in their homes, the same as children from better-off homes.

As to viewing, children from low-income homes were spending from six to seven hours each and every week day watching television, in comparison to four to five hours for children from middle-class homes. The former were more likely to watch television before going to school in the morning, during their noon lunch hour, after school and in the late evening.

As to other mass media usage, both groups spent about an hour each day listening to the radio and about an hour playing records. In terms of newspapers at this age level, they were looked at from three to four times a week by both the poor kids and their middle-class counterparts, but what they looked at were primarily the comics.

In terms of potential impact then, it is television which predominates. Watching television consumed virtually the same amount of time for less advantaged 4th and 5th graders as did the entire school day. Our analysis of the communication behavior of this group then justifiably concentrates on that medium.

Given this devotion to the content of one medium, what kinds of controls exist on their viewing patterns? As might be anticipated, children from poorer homes reported less control over their viewing habits. They were less likely to have a rule about how late they could watch at night, less likely to be told by anyone that there were certain shows they should not watch, and less likely to be punished by not being allowed to watch television. When asked who had the most control in their family over what was watched, they were likely to say "I have."

As interesting or startling as some of these findings may be, I believe that the most important data we have obtained deal with the functions of television for low-income children. Let me begin by talking about the extent to which these youngsters perceived television to portray people and events as true to life. The children were given a series of questions to agree or disagree with, which included:

"The people I see on TV shows are just like people I know in real life."

"The same things that happen to people on TV often happen to me in real life."

"Families I see on TV are like my family."

"The programs on TV tell about life the way it really is."

For each of these items, differences were found which correlated with the poverty background of the child and/or his race. Children raised in disadvantaged environments were far and away more likely to say, "Yes, TV shows it like it is," that these things and people they saw were true-to-life. Low-income kids said this more often than middle-income kids, and black children agreed more so than did white children. This finding is prevalent and significant. Belief in the content of television is high among poor children.

I can at this point only speculate with you as to why this is so. Subsequent research must bear me out before a valid statement can be made. But perhaps you can appreciate the logic of an argument that goes like this: An economically poor child does not get to do very much outside his home, except go to school and watch television. The school he goes to is depressing and filled with children very much like himself in terms of background and economics. The activities of the school are limited. There are fewer trips to art museums, nature hikes, etc. So, his contact with the outside world is limited; his primary contact with the outside world is as mediated by television. He has virtually no other standards of comparison or events against which to check the reality of the television world. Thus, what he sees he may believe to be representative of the "real world."

Such speculation demands more rigorous study than we have done yet.

Now, let me offer a further speculation: When the poor child—who already believes what he sees on television — checks what he sees on television against the reality he knows in his home and neighborhood, it is his own environment — there is some reason to believe, I think—which he may begin to believe is less real. But, as I have said, this latter belief of mine is speculation and has not yet been fully documented. But children from low-income homes *do* believe a great deal of what they see on television to be real, far more than children from middle-class homes. The whys of that have not yet been adequately documented, either.

Let us turn slightly from this question of how realistic the mass media world is for the ghetto youngster to questions of why he watches so much television. Agreement or disagreement was obtained to such items as these:

"I watch TV because I can learn a lot from it."

"I watch TV because I have nothing better to do."

"I watch TV because it excites me."

"I watch TV because you can learn from the mistakes of others."

Children from lower-class families were more likely

than their better-off counterparts to say that they watched television *to learn* about things *not* in school, about new things, about how to solve problems, about how to act, and so on. Black children were more likely to give these same learning reasons than were white youngsters. For these children, television provided a *school-of-life* function.

This was the only function of television that differentiated among these youngsters, in terms of social status differences. When we looked for racial differences, the black children obtained some additional gratifications from television. To wit: they believed it kept them out of trouble, they had nothing better to do, and they did not have to think or work while watching television.

Let us move on in our chronology to Philadelphia where we obtained data from three-hundred ghetto and suburban teenagers, representing low-income whites and blacks and middle-income whites. It will not be necessary to spend much time on this study, for the findings are basically redundant with all we have said about children six to eight years younger.

Both social class and racial differences were found in many of the communication behaviors we studied. Being poor was sufficient to elicit many differences from the middle-class teenagers. Being poor and black usually served to intensify those differences further.

Perhaps an easy way to summarize this information is to put together a composite media day for our three groups of teenagers. The day we have reference to for the teenagers is a Sunday.

For the middle-class, white teenager, his media effort included three and one-half hours of television, two and one-half hours with a radio, an hour playing records, and definitely some newspaper reading. In the past week he looked at three magazines, and in the past month, he caught two movies.

The lower-class white teenager watched another hour of television, to make it four and one-half, and had the same amount of radio-listening and record playing, but was less likely to have done any newspaper reading. He looked at two magazines in the last week, and went to two movies in the last month.

The black teenager spent more than six hours with television, two hours with the radio, one and one-half hours listening to records, and was even less likely to have read the newspaper. He also read fewer magazines and saw fewer movies.

The teenagers received the same set of questions about the reality of television content that were used with the elementary school children. The results were the same. Teenagers from poorer environments were far more likely to believe that television tells it like it is.

From the teenagers, we gathered some additional information about attitudes toward the mass media. We asked them whether they would believe television, radio or the newspaper if they got conflicting reports from each; which they would keep if they could only keep one;

and which news staff on which medium was doing its job best.

If conflicting reports were received, the majority would believe the TV version, with this response even more prevalent among the lower-income youngsters. Two-thirds to three-fourths would keep television if they could only keep one. The TV news reporter was seen as doing his job the best by 65 per cent of the black youngsters, 55 per cent of the lower-class white youngsters, and 45 per cent of the middle-class white youngsters.

Finally, what are the functions of television for these teenagers? The use of television as a means of finding out what life is all about was more frequent among the lower-class respondents than the middle-class ones. This was even more so for the black teenagers than the white, lower-income ones. They were saying:

"I watch TV because I can learn from the mistakes of others."

"I watch TV because I get to know all about people in all walks of life."

"I watch TV because I want to know what's going on in the world."

"I watch TV because it shows how others solve the same problems I have."

A second function that TV had for the low income teenagers was a "kicks" function. They were more likely to agree that watching television served as a means of getting some thrills and excitement.

Now let us determine what happens with the mass

media among adults who live in low-income environments. We will begin with the mass media habits of the average American. This will serve as a basis for comparing the behavior of the other America.

Tom Green is middle-class. Of the 16 hours that he is awake, he gives from one-fourth to one-third of that time—about five hours—to the mass media. The most popular medium is television. His TV set is in use for six hours a day. He himself watches two to two-and-one-half hours each week day. Green also listens to the radio two hours a day. Green typically has one newspaper delivered. That paper is read for almost 30 minutes each day, with the front page, the sports section and the comics consuming most of that time. Green reads one magazine regularly, has probably read or looked through a magazine in the past week, but not enough on any given day to increase the total of five hours he gives to the other mass media daily. Movie-going is also a negligible consumer of time. Green goes to a movie about every three months.

These represent his use of the mass media. What about his attitudes toward the media? They follow a trend which is consistent with the usage pattern. When asked where he gets most of his news about what is going on in the world today, Green replies, "television," more so than any other medium. When asked which of the media he would be most inclined to believe, he says, "television." When asked which medium he would choose if there were only one available, he answers, "television."

Tom Green depends on television for news, for entertainment, for excitement, for information about the world outside his own. However, here is the case our research supports: despite the extent and pervasiveness of Green's dependency on television, the citizen of below-standard income is socially and significantly even more dependent on that medium, for the same and other purposes.

Let me quickly dispose of the question of mass media access or ownership among the population. Ninety-five per cent of the general public owns at least one working black and white TV set; the same percentage of those whose incomes qualify them for Office of Economic Opportunity assistance own at least one working black and white TV set. More than a third of these groups in fact have more than one working set. TV is equally available to all.

Similarly, there is no great difference in access to the other major mass media between the more and less advantaged citizens. Newspapers are delivered daily to two-thirds to three-fourths of low-income homes (compared to 86 per cent of the general public), and those homes have two radios compared to three in the general public). The poor are not media-poor. It is not in terms of access that the media have their potential impact, but in terms of *usage*.

For the low-income American, television is the preponderant, if not quite the sole, source of mass media stimulation. It appears to be his critical link to the outside world of the "haves." He is far less likely than the middle-class citizen to have done any magazine reading lately. He reads the newspaper less frequently, and when he does read it, he reads it less intensively (focusing on the headlines and ads). For six in ten, it has been at least six months since they saw a movie.

What is the television usage? Tom Green and his wife watch television about two hours on a weekday. *The adults in low-income homes in our sample watch TV for five hours each day.*

Let me illustrate this quantity of television exposure in another way. To most Americans, eight hours is regarded as a typical workday. Among the low-income adults interviewed, 25 per cent of them spent eight hours each day with TV (compared to 5 per cent in the general population).

Tom Green gives about one-quarter of his waking day to the mass media. The low-income American spends half of his day with the media, and three-quarters of that is TV time.

Let me now relate this information on how people use the media to the *attitudes* that Americans have about the media. These attitudes are generally predictable from the relative exposure patterns just described.

By typical adults, TV is regarded as the principal information source for general news, world news, political news, etc. At the same time it is far and away favored as the most credible source. It is even more so regarded by low-income Americans. For example, 40 per cent of the general public say they get most of their world news from TV, compared with 70 per cent of the low-income citizens. A majority of the general public would believe what they get from television before they believe what they get from the newspaper. But an even larger majority of low-income citizens hold that view.

So far, these research findings pinpoint the relative dependence of the low-income adult on a single mass medium. They also indicate the relative non-use by the poor of alternative sources of information about the world outside their home and neighborhood.

Let me now characterize the general media content preferences of these adults. In terms of newspaper reading low-income Americans differ from their better-off counterparts in that they appear to use the newspaper as a substitute bulletin board. They focus on the newspaper headlines—seldom going very far into the stories—on the advertisements, and on such things as the obituaries, the weather, and so on.

As for television, shows of adventure, excitement, action and violence are regularly viewed by a much larger proportion of low-income citizens than the general public.

The TV viewing preferences and program choices of low-income white citizens are extremely similar to those of black Americans, and markedly different from those of the general public—with the difference concentrated in the extent of preference for shows of excitement and action.

Let me conclude by saying that this collection of information is more suggestive than definitive. However, the few mass media studies that have been done show more similarities than contradictions. The mass medium of the poor is television. It is a preferred and almost exclusive source of information about the world outside his neighborhood. Without competing information, he thinks the world is like what he sees on TV. And he would question competing information from the other media. His appetite for excitement is nurtured through those things he likes best and watches most of. His relatively greater social isolation (fewer close friends, fewer people to talk to regularly) finds a compatible substitute in television. These are the things we think are being structured for him, on the basis of his uses of mass communication.

CHAPTER TWO

How Does a Metropolitan Daily Newspaper Cover the Inner City?

by
Philip S. Heisler
Managing Editor
The *Baltimore Evening Sun*

HOW DOES A METROPOLITAN DAILY NEWSPAPER COVER THE INNER CITY?

MR. HEISLER has had a long and distinguished newspaper career. He has been managing editor of the *Baltimore Evening Sun* since 1949. Before that he served in the Washington bureau of the *Sunpapers*. In 1943 he went to the Pacific as a foreign correspondent for the *Sunpapers* and Reuters. He was the first editor of the *Sunday Sun Magazine* and news director for WMAR-TV in Baltimore. Mr. Heisler's own city of Baltimore has been one of those torn by urban disorder. In April, 1968, after the assassination of Dr. Martin Luther King, Jr., several days of disorders and rioting in the inner city resulted in injuries to hundreds of persons and the arrest of thousands of others. National Guardsmen and federal troops had to be called in to quell the disorders. Baltimore is typical of many cities in that it has a ghetto with all the attendant evils of the inner-city problem. Because ot this typicality Mr. Heisler was asked to describe the *Sunpapers'* efforts to cover the inner city in Baltimore.

For the past three years newspaper editors have debated long and loudly on the question of how best to report the news of the inner city. After innumerable studies, surveys, reports and speeches, there is less than unanimous agreement not only on *how* they should cover the inner city news but also on *what* the real news is.

Looking back over the annual reports of one national association of editors who have been seriously concerned with this problem, I found a curious sequence of conclusions.

Three years ago this group's report concluded that the media's coverage of the inner city was not bad as many critics made it out to be.

Two years ago the same group's study committee concluded: "A lot has been done but we still have a long way to go."

And this year the report concluded that the inner city presented "a great obligation and opportunity."

At first glance these reports would seem to indicate that newspapers have been losing ground on the inner city problem of communications. Actually, however, this curious sequence of conclusions reflects a changing viewpoint on the precise nature of the problem.

I think we can understand the problem better if we first take a quick look backward into its history and some of the surrounding factors.

The problems of the inner city really began to surface at the end of World War II. The war had brought

HOW DOES A METROPOLITAN DAILY NEWSPAPER COVER THE INNER CITY?

hordes of rural people into the metropolitan cities. Regular housing had been curtailed and temporary shanty centers sprang up. The pressurized density of population was further increased by the new crop of war babies. Neighborhoods and neighbors changed — and the increased pressure of urban living began smoldering in the inner cities. Most newspapers did little about it at that time.

Why?

The answer is that at that particular time the newspapers were frantically busy looking at another problem that was much more visible and seemed much more immediate. At the same time the squeeze was on in the inner city, the flight to the suburbs was on full wing.

Newspapers saw their circulation in the inner city decrease as their regular readers and subscribers moved to the suburbs. As new cities and new towns sprang up in the suburban areas, newspaper editors—quite correctly—saw the need for increased news coverage of the new area with its important problems of housing, planning, zoning, annexation, home rule, etc.

Many newspapers responded to this problem quickly. Staffs were expanded and sent out into the counties. Old city editors got a new title—they became metropolitan editors. Metropolitan sections, Beltway sections, county editions and split-run editions were launched.

Unfortunately, while we concentrated on the very real problem of the expansion into the suburbs, the problem in the inner city smoldered. The winds of change that nurtured the growth of suburbia also fanned the smoldering problems of the inner city and they suddenly burst into flame right under our feet. Again, some newspapers recognized and appraised the situation quicker than others.

Some tried to do something about it. Some tried to ignore it. Those who tried to do something about it did not always come up with instant perfection. There was a sudden rash of articles in many newspapers with headlines like "The Negro in Kitsay County," "Skilled Tradesmen and the Negro," "Job Opportunities and the Negro Woman" and "Negro Cowboys—the Forgotten Heroes of the Wild West."

Of course, that kind of reporting was not the answer. Newspapers were looking *at* the people of the inner city. If there was any communication in the inner city, it was all downward. None of it was coming up.

Editors who recognized the complexity and enormity of the problem of giving meaningful news coverage to the inner city realized that they were not equipped to do a good job immediately, regardless of how much some people demanded action *now*.

At the *Evening Sun* we made a very careful and deliberate study of the problem. We went out and walked the streets and talked to people.

We found that our inner city had changed much more than we expected. We also found that it had changed quite differently from what some instant experts were saying. We found that the spokesmen for the people of the inner city had changed — if, indeed, there had ever been spokesmen. We found that the political forces of the inner city were changing drastically. Real and influential Negro bloc voting finally appeared for the first time in this past election.

We studied readership surveys. And the surveys said some interesting things. For instance, they showed that inner city residents, on the average, read the paper less than residents of other sections and depended on television more for their news.

They showed Negro readership of comics and panels much below that of whites; Negro readership of sports about three-fourths that of whites; and Negro readership of advertising about the same as whites. We learned that more Negro women read the stock tables than white women. One study suggested that it was Negroes *under* 50 years of age who most often referred to stock quotations, but for white readers it was those *over* 50 who most often read the stock quotations.

These surveys also showed us that Negroes in the 18 to 29-year-old age bracket preferred to be called blacks, but that 70 per cent of those over 29 preferred to be called Negroes.

We studied circulation charts and circulation experiences in other cities. We found that circulation service had deteriorated in the inner city. A national survey indicated that some newspapers had actually given up any attempt to maintain any circulation in the ghetto areas. At the very time when real communication was most needed within the inner city the physical means of communication through newspapers was breaking down.

We found that a whole new subgovernment centering around the myriad war-on-poverty projects had been born in the inner city.

We studied the report of the National Advisory Commission on Civil Disorders. We were not so much interested in those sections that dealt with the spot news coverage of riots as we were in the much broader aspects.

I was particularly impressed with two portions of that report. Speaking of the newspapers, that report stated:

> *They have not communicated to the majority of their audience—which is white—a sense of the degradation, misery and hopelessness of living in the ghetto. They have not communicated to whites a feeling for the difficulties and frustrations of being Negro in the United States. They have not shown understanding or appreciation of — and thus have not communicated — a sense of Negro culture, thought or history.*

And later it stated:

> *Many editors and news directors, plagued by shortages of staff and lack of reliable contacts and sources of information in the city, have failed to recognize the significance of the urban story and to develop resources to cover it adequately.*

While we were taking this long, hard look, it became apparent that the traditional organization for covering a city was no longer adequate. The reportorial nucleus of the city staff consisting of individual beats like courts, police, schools, politics and social agencies could not do the job. This may have been good enough for the simple city but in the larger complexes, disjointed reporting of fragments prevented true comprehension of public affairs.

Now we were ready to start covering the inner city as we thought it should be covered.

We sent reporters back to college. To get the expert reporters we needed to cope with the complex inner city we had to provide specialized training. For the past two years we have sent reporters to the Urban Journalism Center at Northwestern University. Here they have undergone a concentrated course of study and field work directed by the country's leading experts in urban problems.

The metropolitan editor—that creature born during the battle of the suburbs — now has a new right hand man—the urban affairs editor. He and his team of urban affairs reporters concentrate their full time on the constantly changing and increasingly complex inner city.

We recruited additional Negro reporters and developed other specially oriented writers from the ranks of volunteer VISTA workers who had worked and studied in the ghetto. With their intimate knowledge of the inner city we were able to open up lines of communication that flowed into the newspaper as well as out from it.

With these specially selected reporters we were able to establish real contacts with the people. We no longer simply covered the National Association for the Advancement of Colored People, the Urban League and the Committee on Racial Equality—but the Black Panthers, Black Muslims and dozens of other organizations as well. Inner city reporters have gotten to know and talk with the welfare recipients as well as the welfare director, the policemen on the beat as well as the district captain, the school kids as well as the school principal, the pool hall operators as well as the swimming pool owners. And, yes, even a dope peddler or two.

This is an intangible kind of thing that can be explained best with an example. Several months ago a woman resident of the inner city was brutally bitten by a police dog while a policeman of the K-9 Corps was investigating an incident. We reported the incident of the biting fully and the next day there was a demonstration outside the district police station demanding that police dogs be taken out of residential districts. Picket lines were formed. Messages and demands were sent to the mayor and governor. Angry groups paraded around police headquarters. Investigations were demanded into the use of police dogs. We reported all of it fully.

After a few days the authorities announced that all police dogs would be pulled out of the inner city residential districts. Again, it was reported fully and the incident seemed closed.

However, two of the reporters who by now have a pretty good feel of the pulse of the inner city told me that the great majority of people of the inner city—the inner city, too, has a silent majority—wanted the police dogs kept on duty patrolling the streets. The biting incident was unfortunate, but the inner city residents—the victims of the great majority of crimes—wanted the police dogs.

They had no spokesman. They staged no demonstrations. But a comprehensive survey of the people on the street showed that the reporter's information was correct. We printed the story, and the dogs are now back on patrol. This is real coverage of one aspect of inner city news.

For years editors have recognized the limitations of the vertical system of covering news. Under this vertical system a reporter assigned to a beat or agency handles all stories that originate or pass through there.

For example, let us consider a simple story such as the planning of a new recreation center in the inner city.

Under the vertical system the story first sees the light of print when the reporter covering the Department of Recreation writes a story announcing plans for the center. The story will next surface when a City Council committee considers the proposal and has a hearing on it. A different reporter, knowing little or nothing about the background, will write this story. Next it will come up in the City Council for action. Again, another reporter will do this story.

Our study of the inner city gave new impetus to implementing the horizontal system of covering news. Under the horizontal system the story will probably first surface when the reporter covering the neighborhood writes a story indicating the need for the center and the neighborhood interest for it. It is now his story and he follows it through — across all beats. He follows it into the Department of Recreation, before the council committtee, into the City Council, and on into the construction and completion stages.

Armed with the background and intimate details that he has, this reporter is able to present a much more detailed, balanced and comprehensive report. To him the proposed recreation center is not just a cold roll of floor plans. He knows the neighborhood where it will be built. He knows the people who will use it. He knows which forces support and oppose it.

While it was not started with the inner city problem specifically in mind, I have found that our "Direct Line" —an "Action Line" type of column—has been one of the most effective (and perhaps least respected) lines of open communication between the inner city people and the newspaper.

The average inner city resident is not a letter-to-the-editor writer. He does not know personally any people on the newspaper, and he is not likely to wander into a newspaper office with his complaint or ideas. But with "Direct Line" he can pick up the telephone and talk to the newspaper. Or he can scribble a note on a postcard and send it to the paper. He does not have to identify himself if he does not want to. He does not have to be grammatical. He is invited to sound off. And he is assured that the newspaper listens.

The frustrating entanglements with bureaucratic red tape in dealing with the Welfare Department, Social Security, Health Department, Veterans Administration and housing authorities are a major problem for inner city residents. They have more than their share of problems and they get more than their share of brush-offs from the bureaucrats. They have found a voice and a friend in "Direct Line." And I have found that more than 60 per cent of the thousands of calls and letters we get every week come from residents of the inner city. It may not be the most sophisticated line of communication, but it is communication that moves both ways. And it works.

To some critics and some newspaper editors the answer to the problem of covering inner city news was simple. They would print the pictures of some Negro brides on the society pages; drop racial labels in identification; put some Negro women's clubs in the club calendar; and do a series of lavishly illustrated articles on soul food or soul music—and then they would consider the job done. Their answer will satisfy only those who do not know the question.

Getting urban affairs specialists and assigning more men to the streets of the inner city is also only a partial answer.

Real news coverage of the inner city is possible only

when the entire staff of a newspaper recognizes the new nature and new challenge of the inner city. For inner city news is reported not only from the streets, it is covered in the governor's office, the mayor's office, the Department of Sanitation, Department of Health, nursing homes, small loan offices, accident wards, and at rock 'n roll concerts.

Inner city news cannot be confined to the news pages. It is on the society pages, sports pages, theater pages, editorial pages and financial pages. And if it is not there—in every section of the paper—the newspaper is not covering the inner city.

And for a newspaper editor or reporter, real coverage of the inner city starts when he stops talking and starts listening—perhaps to a slightly different drummer.

CHAPTER THREE

The Role of the Press in a Continuing Urban Crisis

by
Joseph W. Shoquist
Managing Editor
The *Milwaukee Journal*

THE ROLE OF THE PRESS IN A CONTINUING URBAN CRISIS

MR. SHOQUIST has become one of our leading experts on the subject of covering civil disorders. He has lectured widely on the subject, including appearances at the American Press Institute at Columbia University. He has been a member of the *Milwaukee Journal* staff since 1955. Before that he was with newspapers in Idaho and Montana and also taught journalism at Montana State University. His paper, the *Journal,* is one of the most widely respected newspapers in the United States, besides enjoying dominance and high respect in its own community. Milwaukee has been the scene of urban disorders but it has also been the scene of another kind of event, the 200 nights of racial protest marches led by the Rev. James Groppi in 1967. Most protests and disorders spend themselves in a few days at most. But Milwaukee's was an extraordinary experience—200 nights! It was an extraordinary experience for a newspaper, too, and Mr. Shoquist was asked to discuss just how the press copes with such an extended crisis event.

What is the urban crisis, anyway? Is it racial violence, crime in the streets, or soaring tax rates? Is it crumbling housing, unemployment, clogged freeways, public welfare, or civil rights demonstrations?

The urban crisis is all of these things, and more.

In recent years in Milwaukee, we have seen open housing marches that lasted for 200 consecutive days and frequently were marked by violence.

We had a racial disturbance that virtually paralyzed the city. We have had sit-ins protesting segregation in schools and other issues.

A band of pacifists calling themselves the Milwaukee 14 raided the local Selective Service Office and burned draft records in an incident that involved some of our reporters and photographers unwittingly and caused a public furor.

A storm of controversy has swirled around the Model Cities program almost from the start.

Milwaukee's public schools have been plagued by violence. In the heart of the Negro district, fights, fires and window breaking are a common occurrence in the public schools.

In September, 1969, a group of welfare mothers, led by the intrepid Father Groppi, marched 80 miles from Milwaukee to Madison to protest cuts in public welfare. They invaded the chambers of the state legislature and brought proceedings to a halt before police and National Guardsmen ejected them.

All of this violent and disruptive activity has had a traumatic effect on the community. The average citizen, fearing for his traditions, his institutions and even his safety, is deeply disturbed. Not only his tranquility but his very way of life is threatened. He is resentful and angry, and he wishes someone would do something about it.

Not surprisingly, he has turned on the messenger who brings him the bad news, along with the good, and with mounting impatience he is letting us know how he feels.

The tendency to blame the press for the problems of society is older than the press itself. Alexander the Great beheaded the messengers who brought him news of military defeats. And in "Antony and Cleopatra," when the royal messenger brought Cleopatra the news that Antony had married Octavia, she flew into a rage. As she berated the hapless courier, he blurted out: "Gracious, Madam, I that do bring the news made not the match."

Somehow, the average citizen is convinced that the press is at least partly responsible for our present trouble. If the papers would just ignore it, surely it would go away. After all, don't these people just want attention? Aren't they just looking for headlines?

The most visible of the urban problems, and the one that evokes the greatest amount of public emotion, involves the struggle for racial equality. Ask any editor of a metropolitan newspaper and he will probably tell you that coverage of racial news is the most explosive issue in urban journalism today. Emotions run high on all sides and the editor is caught in the middle. To get an idea of depth of feeling you need only to look at a few letters to the editor. Let me read you a couple, received by my paper.

"Dear Sir," one letter began, "Today is a very happy day for us. We are moving from this putrid and backward city. We will be miles away from the monopolistic *Journal,* the welfare-addicted black scum and a one-horse town. May you have a riot every year."

Another subscriber wrote this note to the editor of the *Journal:* "Dear sir, what is the matter with you—you rotten nigger lover? I pray that we could have a Hitler to give these black devils the gas chamber. That's what they deserve."

I think these illustrate the point that coverage of civil rights activity is controversial and often unpopular with the readers.

The question, then, is what to do about it. It would be easy to follow the advice of one of our readers who wrote as follows:

"In these perilous days of our city's unrest, I call upon you to contribute to the city's welfare, tranquility and good name. Please do Milwaukee the biggest favor you ever have—stop giving Groppi and his tribe of hoodlums any more publicity. Make a public announcement in the press that no more details will be reported on them. Things will quiet down."

We would make a lot of readers happy if we followed such advice. It sounds like an easy solution. But it wouldn't be right, and we know it. And it wouldn't work, either. A newspaper cannot eliminate controversy by ignoring it, for it will not go away just because the press tries to suppress it.

In the long run, the newspaper undoubtedly would suffer if it suppressed news of racial protest. For we cannot forget that our reputation as a newspaper is at stake in coverage of controversy. A newspaper that has spent years building reader confidence in itself may quickly destroy that confidence by suppressing legitimate news.

And what of the moral values? Can a newspaper in good conscience ignore the social issues involved in such a question as civil rights because it doesn't happen to like the spokesman for the cause?

I'd like to describe some of the news situations we have faced and tell how we have tried to cope with them.

Let me preface this with the observation that Milwaukee's problems are probably no more severe than those of other large cities. I would not want to give the impression that we are an embattled city.

But we have been in the public eye more than some places, partly because of the efforts of Father James Groppi. He is the white Catholic priest who has crusaded for open housing and other racial causes.

Much of the controversy over civil rights in Milwaukee swirls around Father Groppi. And much of the criticism of the Milwaukee newspapers concerns our coverage of him.

The fact that we have had a rather continuous series of events involving racial protest has made Milwaukee somewhat of a case study in civil rights activity. And it has created a long series of challenges to editors of the Milwaukee newspapers in deciding how to cover it.

The first rumblings of racial discontent in Milwaukee started in the early 1960's when a small group of black and white militants—the local chapter of CORE—protested de facto segregation of the schools in Milwaukee. Nothing much came of this.

Then Father Groppi, who was the adviser of the local NAACP youth council, launched a campaign against the Eagles club. Father Groppi and his young followers demanded that judges and other public officials resign from the Eagles club because it excluded blacks from membership. They picketed the club and tensions began to rise.

We reported these demonstrations in stories and pictures, with what we thought was good judgment and restraint. We tried to judge each occurrence on its news value and treat it accordingly. Some of the stories made page 1; most didn't.

One night in 1966, Father Groppi and a few dozen of his youth commandos, mostly black, marched to the home of a judge who lived in Wauwatosa, an upper middle class suburb. They picketed the judge's house for a while and then left.

My newspaper decided to play the story down, because we considered it potentially explosive and we didn't want to encourage it. We thought that by minimizing the coverage, we might cool a tense situation. We printed a small story on an inside page.

The demonstrations continued for a few nights. We continued to cover it in a low-key manner. Then TV moved in, with its cameras and lights, and things got out of hand. Crowds of whites formed, stones and other objects were thrown, and violence erupted. Finally, the National Guard had to be called on to put down the disorders. It became a major page 1 story in the *Journal.*

The editors of the *Journal* learned an important lesson from this. We found that playing down news of a racial demonstration does not necessarily discourage it. We determined that thereafter we would report racial conflict as we would any other news.

On July 30, 1967, we had a serious racial disturbance. The National Guard was called out and the mayor imposed a strict curfew. It was a small disturbance compared to Detroit's, which had just occurred, or to Newark and Watts. But it stunned the city, and for the first time, I think, Milwaukeeans really realized the depth of their racial problem.

Naturally, we editors did some soul searching about

it and about our role. Why did it happen in Milwaukee? Could we have averted it? Did we fail to adequately inform Milwaukeeans of the problems that led to the disturbance?

The questions came easier than the answers.

The causes of a racially-related related riot are too complex to be readily isolated and identified. You cannot just point your finger and say that this was the reason, or that was the cause. It isn't that simple.

A riot does not begin with a speech by a black militant or an incident with police. It does not stem from a civil rights march or a dispute over open housing.

It develops slowly, over the years, before it finally occurs. Its origins are in the despair of the ghetto dweller and in the failure of whites to comprehend and respond. I will not try to explain this sociologically—I doubt that I could—but as a newspaper editor I am deeply concerned about it and about the role of the press in this urban problem.

I am not referring merely to coverage of a riot. To me, that presents no great problem in editorial judgment. You cover a big riot just as you would any major story, with all the resources you can command.

The paper's responsibility in a riot is to be a stabilizing influence by reporting the event fully. Public safety demands this. If we leave a vacuum, we invite the rumormongers to move in. Of course the newspaper must use good judgment and restraint and not add to the problem, but, given a modicum of good sense, this is not difficult.

The real challenge to the urban editor is in interpreing the many facets of city life that lead to rioting. It is one thing to send out a platoon of writers and photographers to report violence in the street; it is another to report the social stresses that we live with, day in and day out.

How, for instance do you convey the sense of hopelessness of the black man, without alienating your white readers? How does a newspaper with a largely white staff even begin to report the black community, which distrusts the paper and is suspicious of its motives?

A conversation I had with a young black man who works in the ghetto in my city stands out vividly in my mind. He argued that the majority of Milwaukee's 100,000 Negroes—the poorest and the blackest of the blacks—don't read the *Milwaukee Journal* and couldn't care less about what it says or thinks.

"You simply are not relevant to the ghetto black man," he told me. "You are economically and socially oriented away from him, and what you write does nothing to extend his existence. The black man has lost his trust and faith in the established press and doesn't believe you want to serve him. You might as well forget him."

These are discouraging words to an editor of a paper that has made an effort to understand the black community and to report it on some kind of equal terms.

I am sure my friend is at least partly correct. I like to think that our white readers benefit from the knowledge of the Negro community that we give them, and that perhaps the black man's image is better because of it.

But I believe we are going to have to find ways to reach the black reader if we are to contribute to a lasting solution to the urban crisis. Whether he likes to admit it or not, the black man *does* need us. He needs the information and the enlightenment that we provide, just as the white reader needs it.

The problem of reaching the black reader is not just one of editorial rapport. The physical problem of getting the paper to black people and collecting for it is itself discouraging. But I don't think this is a sufficient reason to throw up our hands and say, what's the use?

I cannot agree with a metropolitan editor who said recently that circulating the paper to the black reader is not worth the trouble it takes because the black man has no buying power anyway. Even from a purely *economic* point of view, this would seem a shortsighted attitude; viewed in a broader perspective—that of the necessity to inform the citizenry—it is entirely unacceptable.

Reaching the black man, then, is part of the problem in urban journalism. I cannot offer an easy solution. I don't think there is one. Hiring more black reporters may help. A determination on the part of the editors to report the black community and to see that black people are properly represented in the paper is unquestionably required.

But if we are to acquire black readers, and avoid losing our white readers in the process, it is going to take effort and patience. Probably we are going in the right direction—to report the black community as completely and fairly as we can and take our lumps from those who object.

At a more immediate level though, we are faced with the problem of covering continuing demonstrations which cause so much controversy among our readers.

We got a real taste of this in Milwaukee after the disturbance of 1967, when Father Groppi and his youth commandos conducted the longest continuing racial demonstration in the city's history. Their object was the passage of an open housing ordinance in Milwaukee.

They staged nightly marches to press their demands. One night, when Father Groppi and his followers marched into the south side of Milwaukee—a white, working class section of the city — violence broke out. It was 1966 all over again.

This time we reported the violent incidents as the major stories they were. We also reported the views of people on both sides of the issue, and of those in the middle.

Much pressure was exerted on us to suppress coverage of Father Groppi and the open housing marchers. Merchants feared for their business and city officials worried about the city's image. Our own business office was concerned about what was happening to the city. Our mail from readers ran heavily against the demonstrators.

We started to have a lot of trouble with Henry Maier, the mayor of Milwaukee, as a result of our coverage of these demonstrations. Over and over again he demanded that we ignore Father Groppi and the housing marches.

We didn't ignore Father Groppi, but neither did we ignore the mayor, who vigorously opposed a city-only open housing law. He wanted one that covered the entire metropolitan area, and we gave his views much publicity.

We chose not to suppress Father Groppi because we believed he was making legitimate news and that the viewpoint he represented deserved to be heard. The fact that it was not popular with the majority of our readers, or with the mayor, was not sufficient reason to cut him out of the news columns. And, of course, even if it wanted to, a newspaper couldn't suppress news of a demonstration marked by violence that involved thousands of people. Television and radio were there, and so were the people who witnessed and participated in it. They knew what was happening.

The marches went on for 200 days, and they caused us a lot of concern and travail. How do you handle a situation that continues for 200 days and is potentially explosive? We handled it this way. For the first few weeks, when the incidents were newsworthy and when large crowds turned out for the demonstrations, we reported them with pictures and stories and treated them as the major news they were — page 1 stories, usually. But, as the weeks wore on, they lost their news value and our coverage diminished — deliberately, to a certain extent. We kept track of them, but after a while they didn't get much attention — just a paragraph or two on most days.

Father Groppi and the youth council eventually won their battle. After the mayoral elections of 1968, the mayor suddenly decided that Milwaukee needed an open housing ordinance after all, and the Common Council passed one that covered all housing in the city. What had seemed like an impossible hurdle only months before now was easily accomplished. I think many Milwaukeeans must have wondered, after it was all over, why it had been such an issue in the first place.

Throughout the marches and the mayoral campaign, the mayor attacked the *Milwaukee Journal* in press releases and public speeches. He demanded and got free time from the local television stations, including the one owned by the Journal Company, for a series of half-hour programs in which he blasted the *Journal.* As a campaign issue, the "evils" of the *Milwaukee Journal* were second only to the "evils" of Father Groppi.

We opposed the mayor's position on open housing and endorsed his opponent for election.

The mayor was re-elected overwhelmingly. He got more than 80 per cent of the vote, the largest majority ever received in a mayoral election in Milwaukee. I guess that if it proved nothing else, it showed that the power of the press is not limitless, despite what some politicians might have you believe.

The open housing crisis has passed and Father Groppi has turned to other pursuits, equally unpopular, but our difficulties with Mayor Maier have continued.

After Father Groppi, the issue became the Model Cities program. The circumstances were different, but the script was familiar. The mayor insisted that we ignore an organization of black residents called Triple O who opposed his plan for carrying out Model Cities. We didn't because we thought that they represented a significant segment of opinion in the black community and deserved to be heard. We did, however, support the mayor's program for Model Cities.

The mayor renewed his crusade against the *Journal*. He refused to speak to any reporters in Milwaukee. Instead, he held a weekly press conference on television—which was mostly a half-hour tirade against the *Journal*.

Our reaction to most of this was to turn the other cheek. We faithfully reported the mayor's attacks on us along with his other statements. Occasionally we refuted some of his more outrageous misstatements and distortion. But mostly, we continued to cover him as a mayor should be covered and let the public draw its own conclusions about the merits of his charges.

Our difficulties with the mayor of Milwaukee were not unique. Newspapers in Los Angeles, Honolulu and Minneapolis have had much the same problem with their mayors. Undoubtedly there have been others around the country.

The situation is understandable. Urban officials are a frustrated and unhappy lot, for good reason, and it's not surprising that they should try to transfer some of the blame for urban problems to the press.

An editor may not relish this role, but he accepts it. And most of us have developed thick skins. We realize that we really can't do much about the political byproducts of urban conflict, except endure them and try to keep our good humor.

We have outlasted more than one despot while continuing to do what we think is right, and we will outlast many more.

The main challenge confronting the urban press, as I see it, is to maintain balance and perspective in covering what is essentially negative news. We must take care not to present a distorted picture of urban society, while we continue to report honestly what is going on in our communities. To do the former requires good judgment and good sense; to accomplish the latter calls for determination and courage.

I think the public, in its heart, understands our role —that we must report what is happening. We have to reflect society as it is, not as we wish it were. We must make clear what the challenges are, and identify those who challenge us. It is our historic role, and a proper one, to report violence and turmoil along with good news.

Like it or not, the press does report what happens in America. And if Americans do not like what we report, then perhaps it is America that needs changing, not the press.

CHAPTER FOUR

What Can Broadcasters Do to Break the Inner-City Communication Barrier?

by
William Monroe, Jr.
Washington Editor
NBC "Today" Program

WHAT CAN BROADCASTERS DO TO BREAK THE INNER-CITY COMMUNICATION BARRIER?

As a reporter for the broadcast media, Mr. Monroe has been very active in coverage of urban affairs and civil disorders. His editorials on school desegregation for WDSU-TV won a Peabody Prize. He is a past president of the Radio-Television News Directors Association and the Radio-Television Correspondents Association. Before taking over as Washington editor for the NBC "Today" program, he was NBC's news bureau chief in the nation's capital. Because radio and television are the media to which the poor of the inner city seem to have the easiest access and in which they have the greatest interest, Mr. Monroe was asked to discuss what these very important and pervasive media could do about the crisis in urban communication.

On May 9, 1970, I was in the nation's capital in an eighth-floor corner suite of the Washington Hotel overlooking 15th Street. The huge crowd of war protestors was jamming the street below, moving from the Ellipse, where they had just been listening to speeches, toward H Street, where they would turn left toward the one edge of Lafayette Square that was legally open to them. A cameraman was leaning out of the hotel window to shoot film of the spread-out human mass. And a soundman was poking his microphone out of the window to pick up a chant that was reverberating between the buildings with the kind of deep and primitive noise that a waterfall makes.

I couldn't help but reflect that, for a scene of relatively simple ingredients, it presented a remarkably subtle and complex problem of communication.

With an advance apology, I want to be specific about the crowd's chant. The crowd's meter, if basic, was effective: "One, two, three, four, we don't want your fucking war." They obviously enjoyed it. It was a roar, repeated endlessly.

What were they saying? Were they petitioning the President of the United States, or cursing him, or both at the same time? Could a petition delivered with a curse be effective?

The crowd, 99 per cent of it, was remarkably peaceful. So were the Washington cops. The non-violence on both sides was impressive.

But I couldn't help but think that, if the students did

expect to get through to Mr. Nixon, they were using the wrong language. To the President, inevitably, there had to be a blast of harshness, an edge of violence if you will, in those words. He could hardly have reacted with any positive emotions to words he could only look on as obscenities, as expressions of irrationality, as a negation of dialogue, as an organized tantrum. The language *did* express anger. Maybe they wanted Mr. Nixon to *feel* that anger. Maybe the expression of anger in some situations is an end unto itself.

I couldn't help but think also of the NBC soundman faithfully recording, with excellent quality, language that would not be issuing from anybody's television set. I kidded him to the effect that, if he were a good soundman, he would take care of the problem on the spot by blowing into the mike at the appropriate moment to make the chant come out: "One, two, three, four, we don't want your pfffft war."

But how *is* broadcasting going to tell it like it is? A hundred thousand people thundered this language around Washington for hours. At least tens of thousands of spectators heard them, probably including President Nixon, Mrs. Nixon and Tricia Nixon. But any television station that passed that dialogue on to its viewers would be in trouble with the Federal Communications Commission. And there is a further academic but interesting question, which goes back to what impact the obscenity format might have had on the President: whether a television station which broadcast that chant, as part of its news reporting, would have been helping or hurting the antiwar movement. Not that a television station is supposed to broadcast news, or withhold it, depending on whether that news might help or hurt the peace movement, racial understanding or anything else. In our kind of government, unlike the kind you have today in, say, Greece or Russia, the media are not supposed to shape the news flow according to what *they* have decided is good or bad for the country, or according to what the government thinks is good or bad. The media are supposed to pass along what is interesting and what is important to the people, and let them decide what is good or bad and where the nation ought to go.

But the matter of what protesters are actually *saying*, and the matter of what *effect* television reporting actually has, are complicated questions. And the questions about how the media should deal with the events, the language, the tumult of the racial struggle are equally complex.

Let me start out by indicating some of the real limitations that affect television if anybody is looking to it to save the racial soul of this country.

First of all, we have got to accept the fact that commercial television is a medium of mass entertainment and news. It is a sort of elephant. It cannot be changed by wishful thinking or exhortation into a tiger or a mule. It cannot be converted, as some intellectuals would like, into a sort of thundering liberal church. Its audience of "Bonanza" fans would resist conversion into a congregation and its economic foundation would melt away. It cannot be converted anytime soon, and hopefully never, into a faithful beast of burden for the government, providing endless evenings of free time for congressional candidates and docile reporting of Pentagon handouts and White House briefings. Despite the Agnew criticism and its popularity, the television audience would not like David Brinkley as a flack for the government, and the strong tradition of independent journalism in this country is not ready to give way.

Some people would like television to abandon its logical role as a communicator, as a reflector of American society and a reporter of the American scene; to become involved, to get in there and fight. This is not going to happen. Nor should it happen. There is room for opinion on television in local station editorials and individual commentary. There is room for journalistic dedication and excellence. But there is no room for the NBC board to decide on a particular policy as wise for the nation and then set about selling that policy to the country. It is not up to television to hire squads of experts and start planning for the nation. That will remain up to the government and the institutions which have experts and can influence the government.

Television has no choice but to tend to its duty of keeping the home screen open to the clash of ideas that evenutally shapes American policy. It must *reflect* the currents of thought in the nation, cover the news, facilitate communication between groups, between government and people, between people and government, between black and white, communication among professors and businessmen and students and bureaucrats and consumers and union men. Television cannot step out of character to begin thinking of itself as an institution with answers, as a medium with a message. If it did, it could not perform effectively its profound role as a communicator.

Second, if television *could* set out to sell the nation, or to brainwash it, on ideas of its own, it would almost certainly turn out not to have the miracle powers, or monstrous capabilities, that some attribute to it. It could not, as some seem to think, turn fundamental attitudes around overnight.

There is nothing that changes more slowly than basic human attitudes. The literature of psychiatry tells us that, in a typical case, a psychoanalyst may meet a patient for three days a week, 50 minutes a day, for four or five years. This is *two-way* communication, an expert and his patient, listening and talking, reacting to each other, producing an intense conversation directed right *at* the patient's attitudes. When the process is over, the patient has changed some of his feelings toward himself and the world around him to an extent that he can cope with his problems more easily—but the changes are so subtle his friends may not even notice them.

The television box does not allow a two-way conversation. It is not directed at an individual but at a mass audience. Television can sell a man a tube of Crest toothpaste, especially when it has the American Dental Association vouching for it, but even if it could turn *all* its energies toward the task, and even if you could make the audience pay attention while it did so, it could not on its own, for example, wipe out racism in this country in the next decade or so.

Well, what *can* television do?

It can report the news with sensitivity and awareness so that new ideas, new plans, new proposals, new techniques for dealing with the nation's racial problem can become known, can spread around, can get a chance to grow. And, while it is doing that, it will, of course, also be reporting on the opposition to those new ideas, plans, proposals and techniques, because it has a duty to do so and it is a duty that makes sense. Nothing gets accepted in this country without the opposition being reckoned with and persuaded or somehow accommodated.

And, on the entertainment side of television, the medium can continue its movement toward full inclusion of the black man — not just a singer and dancer but as the model in the commercial and the star of an occasional program.

I am not going to dwell on the entertainment side because my knowledge of it is limited. But it is important. We are, perhaps, halfway between the television of a few years ago where the black man, unless he played a trumpet, was seldom seen — and the television of a few years from now where the black man will be on the scene in a more natural, less self-conscious kind of way.

A lot of blacks laugh and make jokes these days

about Diahann Carroll playing "Julia." They say they do not know any blacks who live like that. But that is missing the point. Ninety per cent of the *whites* on television are fantasy figures also. They have plush apartments and race around in sports cars and, in the commercials, the ladies take bubble baths in the rear seats of limousines while on their way to the opera.

So the problem is, is it better to have some black faces among these unreal characters or not?

TV Guide recently had a piece about Clarence Williams, the 29-year-old actor who was brought up by his grandmother in Harlem and now plays a black cop on "Mod Squad."

Today, whenever Clarence Williams appears around high school kids, and particularly black high school kids, he creates a sensation. About that, he says: "It's kind of nice for kids to see a reflection of themselves. I enjoy being an image of something positive. I want the black kids, and the white kids too, to say, wow, I enjoy him, I'd like to try that."

The process of making the black a life-size part of the entertainment and commercial side of television is underway.

On the news side, it may be useful to look back 10 or 15 years to something I believe television contributed to. I suggest that television—television news—had a vital part in spreading the word of the early sit-ins and freedom rides—the electrifying word that American blacks had quit *asking* and had started *demanding*.

The sheer guts of the people who mounted those primitive, non-violent protests came through in those television pictures and in the ugly sounds of conflict. It came through in the newspapers like a far-off stringed instrument. But it came through on television with all the urgency and all the masculinity of a close-by trumpet. Fade out Louis Armstrong. Fade in Miles Davis.

I was in New Orleans, my home city, when those pictures began coming through. Believe me, the white people and the blacks in that part of the country knew something was happening when those pictures appeared. And the white people hated those pictures. They blamed television for them. They blamed the messenger. They somehow decided those things would not have been happening if the camera hadn't been there to record them and to send those damnable scenes around the country —much in the same manner as we have Vice President Agnew and many others concluding that the damnable scenes of student violence would not be happening today except for that worst of "outside agitators," television, being there to pick them up.

Actually, those anti-television voices may have a point, though less of a point than they believe. Television did not *invent* angry blacks or angry students. But it did give them a way to make themselves heard that was more effective than any previous vehicle of protest. And, not unnaturally, they used it. And they *are* using it. And effective means of protest may, of course, mean the saving of a nation, not the destruction of it.

It would be my guess that television, simply because it was an effective reporter, accelerated the forward motion of American blacks.

But, an important point: television did not do this by making any conscious decision that the nation needed to go in a particular direction. It did it in exercising its normal function as reflector and reporter. In the tradition of American journalism that it took from the print medium, from which most of its earliest newsmen came, television simply decided that the sit-ins and freedom rides were interesting and important, they were news, and so they should be reported on the news programs. Television was not crusading. It was reporting. Jim Clark became news—and Bull Connor, Martin Luther King, and Stokeley Carmichael. They *should* have become news, and they *did*, and that act of reporting, facing up to what was happening, not shrinking away from it, helped push the country along.

Today we face a much less clear-cut situation. By every index, blacks are better off than they were 10 or 15 years ago, but more dissatisfied—an equation we are now familiar with. The legal forms of racism are in the process of disappearing. Thus the forms of racism that remain are much more subtle, more intermeshed with other factors, such as class factors and class feelings. The black struggle is expressing itself occasionally in terms of white racism. In other words, black racism, Why not? There is a backlash from working class whites who have a sense of struggle of their own. And superimposed on top of all of this is the disease of Vietnam.

What can television do about it in the 1970's?

I have no basic formula other than the one we started out with: report it, all of it. Seek out what is interesting and what is important—both what is obviously important and what is potentially important—and put it on the air: the scenes, the clashes, the faces, the speeches, the interviews, and the election nights. Do this in the faith of the Old Testament, politically speaking, that the country will sort out what makes sense, discard what does not, and make the necessary decisions to move ahead. Television must serve up the raw material of information and ideas and emotional climate. But television is not going to solve America's racial problems. America is going to solve America's racial problems.

This is not to take television off the hook. This is not to say that television is doing fine and all we need is more of the same. We need better than that.

We need more black editors, producers and network vice presidents. I would hate to guess at what the figures are in those categories right now. The need is recognized, and those figures will change.

We need more awareness of racial problems on the part of the white editors, producers and vice presidents now running the news organizations and news programs. There is a question I would like to see militant groups ask broadcast news executives just as often as they ask questions about black employment: How often do you have regular contact, regular discussions, with black groups or black leaders? How long has it been since you spent an afternoon talking to people in Harlem, or Anacostia, or along Baltimore's Pennsylvania Avenue?

In that connection, *Columbia Journalism Review* recently commended the *Philadelphia Bulletin* "for its continuing staff seminars with representatives of neighborhoods and community groups, to help sensitize editors and reporters to problems of the inner city."

Broadcasters do some of that, too, but undoubtedly not enough. They ought to consult not only black groups on a regular basis but white blue-collar groups as well, because most news executives live a life isolated from *all* low-income classes, black and white. And we have discovered that it is a mistake to leave lower-income whites out of the racial equation, as both politicians and journalists did without realizing it during most of the Kennedy-Johnson years.

We need to recognize that, while the country is stymied for money during the Vietnam war, it need not declare a moratorium on *thinking* about its racial problems. Daniel Patrick Moynihan's phrase, "benign neglect," may provide a philosophical justification for the politics of an administration that is willing to continue putting its money into Vietnam and its political energy into beating George Wallace. "Benign neglect" cannot provide a comfortable philosophical shield for journalists who would like some relief from the combat fatigue of racial coverage.

Television, in recognition of its journalistic size and

responsibility, should take the lead in seeking out the new things that are interesting, that are important, or potentially important, in the racial kaleidoscope — new things that are happening among the blacks; the Panthers (who are they?); separatism; the lack of recognized national leaders; and, meanwhile, back at the ranch, the NAACP and the Urban League.

Also, new things that are happening among the whites; the "racial" fears of the white union man, part of which turn out to be class fears; the anatomy of prejudice; the argument over busing and, underneath it according to Gallup, the increasing acceptance of school integration; the effect on whites, constructive and destructive, of loud black anger; the demand for law and order, legitimate and illegitimate.

Also, new things are happening in the universities. What are the black students doing? The white students? What are the researchers coming up with about where we stand in the American racial confrontation and what can be done?

In other words, television should not be so arrogant as to try to figure out for itself what should be done. But it should be alert to the possibilities that are being churned up by American society. And it should take up the novel ones, the interesting ones, before they get outshouted in our marketplace of ideas and spread them around so that, whatever they are worth, they do not get lost for lack of exposure.

In doing so, networks and stations can afford to go beyond the kind of normal news coverage they usually practice. Instead of picking up things that are visibly becoming news, they can hire specialists to go looking for things in the racial field that are about news and give currency to some of these happenings ahead of *The New York Times*. This is happening now to an extent, but it could happen more often. They can hire roving editors, sociologists, young journalists—the exact background is not important—to locate happenings that can be developed into hard news and soft news for the evening newscasts and the magazine-type programs. Investigative reporting—in other words, digging—not in the crime and corruption field, but in the racial field.

In the process, there will be some reporting that will shake up and possibly anger whites. There will also be reporting that will shake up and possibly anger blacks—the latter requiring more honesty and nerve in 1970 than the former. We cope easily, as journalists, with the racial excesses of whites. We have the feeling, at least, of being on familiar ground. But white journalists do not cope with confidence with the racial excesses of blacks, and black journalists, unless they identify with the excesses and thus can't even see them, are equally uncertain how to report on them.

Here again, let me inject a caution to the effect that I am not advocating converting the elephant into a tiger. I am not suggesting multiple hours of prime time documentaries worth so many gold stars from the Federal

Communications Commission and so many Dupont awards in compensation for a lost audience. I am suggesting more sensitivity to our racial crisis; more awareness, more energy focused on it by executives, editors and specialists; more ahead-of-the-pack reporting. I would expect to see the most effective examples of it in the networks' evening newscasts and in the local station newscasts. These are the news programs that have the substantial audiences day in and day out. And some sensitive and alert reporting is, indeed, showing up on them.

Television is probably a little smug, a little prone to liberal righteousness in its self-image of doing the decent thing about race, and a little more isolated in suburbia than it thinks it is. But, at the same time, it has not turned its back on the racial struggle and it is doing some worthwhile things — with both predictable and unpredictable results.

You know, over the past few years, television has put on a lot of what I would call "confrontation" documentaries. These are distinguished by angry blacks gesticulating at and loudly accusing local whites who, as the program progresses, get angry themselves. These documentaries have been produced in good faith by people who wanted to help things along by telling it like it is. The theory was that the blacks should have their inning at fussing at whites and whites should know how angry blacks are. Maybe they did some good; I am not sure. Sometimes I think that, next to the urban riots and crime, they did as much as anything else to sanctify black belligerence and to scare the hell out of middle class whites.

I got so I didn't go out of my way to tune in such documentaries. Another name for them could be, "Man, look at what a horrible problem we got" documentaries. They are all problem and no answers. After you have seen one, you can only go out and get drunk. We have seen some documentaries like that lately on pollution. They open and close, in color, on acres of sewage floating on Lake Erie.

A few months ago, out of a sense of duty, I tuned in a CBS documentary that I really did not have much hope for. It was titled, right in the tradition of confrontation documentaries, "The Battle of East St. Louis." It went beyond anger to say something.

It showed a sensitivity-training experiment involving 18 persons, blacks and whites. They included a police sergeant who had been charged three times with brutality —one of the burliest small-town-sheriff-looking cops you have ever seen. There was also a black militant who had been arrested six times, including once or twice by the sergeant.

Three days of sensitivity sessions were condensed into an hour's program. And the harsh verbiage that went back and forth, probing, trying to reach the individuals under the stereotypes, finally got through. Before your eyes, these people started out bitter toward each other and gradually reached the beginnings of some acknowledged respect for each other. And the program wound up with film shot six months later showing that the effects lasted, that the improved understanding was still there, that the cop had learned something about the humanity of the militant and vice versa.

This program could hardly do for television viewers what the three intense days of enforced togetherness did for the participants in East St. Louis. But no black, no white, was likely to watch it without some increased awareness that racial walls can be breached.

This was television operating effectively as a reporter.

On ABC just this week there was an unpretentious little gem of a documentary, 30 minutes long, called "The Eye of the Storm." It was about a third-grade teacher in Riceville, Iowa, who decided, after the death of Martin Luther King, that she wanted to demonstrate somehow to her all-white class of eight-year-olds how prejudice worked.

So she divided her class up into brown-eyed and blue-eyed. One day the brown-eyes became second-class citizens. The next day the blue-eyes tried it. On the day the brown-eyes were down, the teacher invited the kids to accept the idea that brown-eyed people were inferior, slow, less cultured. They had to sit in the back of the room and had to use paper cups at the drinking fountain. Whenever the teacher found fault with them, she linked their defect to their brown-eyed status. The blue-eyed children immediately started lording it over their unhappy classmates. The brown-eyed children were immediately affected by this arbitrarily imposed inferiority: they took twice as long as usual to call out answers to a pack of phonetic cards. After a fight, the teacher asked a brown-eyed boy if he had hit a blue-eyed boy. The answer was: "I hit him in the gut. He called me brown-eyes. They always call us that." After it was over, another brown-eyed youngster said, "You felt like you didn't even want to do anything." The next day the blue-eyed children experienced the same feelings. Arguments and fights went way up. One blue-eyed child said that, during his day of deprivation, he felt "like a dog on a leash." The teacher wound up by tying in their experience with the feelings of American minorities.

This is where it is at — holding up attitudes to the light where people can see them, and thus changing them bit by bit. The sensitivity training expert in East St. Louis and the teacher in Riceville, Iowa, are getting at the problem. Television can help by reporting on *them.*

There is more of this going on than meets the eye, incidentally, and television probably ought to be doing more reporting on it than it is doing. There is a Baltimore group called Prejudice Anonymous representing different religious faiths and races. It talks out problems of prejudice before school and civic groups. In the window of my local hardware store last weekend I noticed a hand-lettered poster advertising a series of four white-black discussion sessions at a neighborhood Catholic school.

Chuck Stone, the black militant writer and former aide to Adam Clayton Powell, has something interesting going on the "Today" show. I am involved in it as sort of straight man. Stuart Schulberg, the producer, originated the idea of having Chuck come on about every three weeks and give a three-minute report, whatever he wants to say on current racial problems. After he is done, the camera picks me up sitting next to Chuck and I ask him questions on what he has just said.

Chuck has castigated Nixon and Agnew, he has questioned the nature of the legal campaign against the Panthers, he has attacked the United States as a violent nation. On one occasion he surprised everybody by *praising* the administration's "Philadelphia Plan." Last week he outraged a good many people by insisting that the Vietnam and Cambodia operations were basically founded on American racism.

After he gets through, leaving God knows how many white television fans poised to throw ash trays at their TV sets, I come on, necessarily, as the house white-man: "Now, Chuck, you don't really mean to say that . . ." And sometimes Chuck grins and admits that maybe he did lay it on a little thick.

This format is basically a platform for an articulate black militant with his message tempered by follow-up questions from a white newsman. Chuck, in effect, is a black commentator on national television. Letters to both of us also indicate that many whites who are not comfortable with Chuck's opinions nevertheless listen to him.

This has just a little, not much but a little, in common with the all-black programs most visible on public television—the programs produced, researched, written, filmed and narrated by blacks. I notice that WNEW in New York is about to begin a Saturday afternoon newscast described as commercial broadcasting's first regularly scheduled all-black television news program. I confess to mixed feelings about trying to combat newscasts that may be subconsciously biased by balancing with newscasts that are consciously biased. But nothing comes easily these days, and probably they are necessary.

In the meantime, television and other media are going to have to face up to things that blacks don't want to hear as well as to the things that are unpleasant to whites. I'm talking about the present one-sidedness of the debate that results from the syndrome of white guilt and black righteousness, the idea that whites can do no right and blacks can do no wrong. This syndrome has resulted in an indignation among whites in one-bathroom homes that has some legitimacy to it and that is not wholly attributable to racism. And it has resulted in some demagoguery among black leaders—the political necessity for each new leader to out-militate his predecessor—tendencies that are fairly characterized in some instances as black racism.

If we build up out of proportion the specter of white racism, we may be cruelly denying to the man in the ghetto the chief tool he needs for improvement — the sense of his own responsibility.

Again, I'm not talking about television *preaching*. I am talking about the reporting of what is happening and what is being said by people who are qualified to speak.

Representative Shirley Chisholm talked to a largely black audience in Washington recently. She talked feelingly about the naturalness of the drive for black power and urged whites to listen to responsible black leaders. She also warned blacks against putting the blame for their condition on "everybody else in society."

Professor Edward Banfield of Harvard, in his book *The Unheavenly City,* suggests that there is today an overemphasis on racism and prejudice. He suggests that prejudice has already declined to a point where it is no longer the major barrier to progress. He suggests that blacks are now in a position to begin the upward thrust that other American ethnic groups achieved before them, and in fact they have begun it. But, he says, if those blacks still at the bottom are told that prejudice is greater than it is, and thus made to feel that it is insuperable, they will suffer defeat more in the face of imagined rather than real racism.

I would like to see television get hold of *more* of the story of this country's racial struggle. It is not easy and it will not make us popular with anybody. Nor should that concern us. We used to wait for the story to come to us. We have a greater tendency today to go out and look for it, but we could do more looking. So, basically, what television can do for the man in the ghetto is to provide an attentive job of reporting on the dialogue and the events leading to a continued decline of racism. That reporting will help accelerate the decline of prejudice.

Part of television and print reporting should involve a watch on how much racism *has* declined and *is* declining. If the prejudice remaining is allowed to be exaggerated, the low-income black man can use that as a cop-out. With prejudice diminished, he is going to have to depend primarily on his own efforts to overcome the still formidable class barriers, as the Jews, the Irish and the Poles did ahead of him. But with the idea still prevalent that prejudice remains a high wall, he will not have the incentive to start tackling the barriers of class. And, whether it is just or unjust, the fact that those class barriers may derive historically from racism does not remove the necessity for him to provide the chief push if he is going to get over them. In other words, if you are going to make a man feel sorry for himself, be sure the facts are with you, because otherwise you are likely to be doing him a disservice.

At the same time, I don't look on this job ahead for television as mechanical or unfeeling, a role without vision, commitment, or faith.

My own conviction is that this is going to be—I am not sure just when— the first great, unified, multiracial nation. I have a feeling that the stubborn, prideful black American of 1970 is the best thing that has happened to the United States since 1776. And right alongside him as a long-range asset is the militant chicano. I see no basic reason, on the other hand, to despair of the fashionably discounted middle American, the white working man who, out of his own deep sense of work and struggle, has felt jostled by the oncoming black but who is making room for him nevertheless.

All we got in 1776 was a pretty good embryo. The American *nation* is being born right now in front of our eyes. Television should go after this story that is so tremendous it is hard to see.

CHAPTER FIVE

What Can the Black Communicator Do to Break the Inner-City Communication Barrier?

by
John H. Johnson
Publisher and Editor
Ebony Magazine

MR. JOHNSON is president of the Johnson Publishing Company and publisher and editor of *Ebony, Tan, Jet* and *Black World* (formerly *Negro Digest*) magazines. He is one of the outstanding black communicators in the country and has also won several awards as one of the nation's outstanding black businessmen. He began to build his publishing operations when he founded *Negro Digest* in 1942. In 1945 *Ebony* followed and has since become the leading magazine for blacks in the country. Mr. Johnson has been widely active in civil rights organizations and has been designated by two presidents to represent the United States at independence ceremonies for African nations. Because of his dual role as a magazine publisher and as a black communicator his thoughts were particularly pertinent to attacking the problem of urban communication.

That communicator of many words and much wisdom, George Bernard Shaw, once confessed: "In moments of crisis, my nerves act in a most extraordinary way. When disaster seems imminent, my whole being is simultaneously braced to avoid it. I size up the situation in a flash, set my teeth, contract my muscles, take a firm grip on myself, and, without a tremor, always do the wrong thing."

All of us at one time or another have suffered through the very human experience that Shaw describes. It is true that crisis situations have often sabotaged our efforts at clear analysis and drawn from us the wrong response. Those of us in mass communications see evidences of this almost daily. It is appropriate, therefore, that we who aspire to become eyes in the perpetual hurricane of events should be examining "The Crisis in Urban Communication," and in particular, that aspect of the problem having to do with the role of the black communicator. His role was shaped largely by the historic development of the black press. Therefore, let me turn to a bit of journalism history.

Until recently in the nation's life, blacks were either ignored by the white press or treated as minstrels, caricatures of human beings or common criminals. In articles, stories, anecdotes, cartoons and "nigger-in-the-woodpile" jokes, black men were made to appear superstitious, happy-go-lucky, improvident, lazy and immoral. They were portrayed as liars, thieves and drunkards. There was little in the white press to give its readers the impression that blacks were born under respectable circumstances, attended schools, achieved in various fields of endeavor, that they had beautiful women, or, for that matter, that they ever died. Most of the white press treated them as creatures of another America — dark, dangerous, foreboding and best forgotten. In fact, for many years an unwritten rule in the South decreed that a black man's picture could not appear in a newspaper unless it was in connection with a crime.

And so it came to pass that black America—shoved into a corner of the national scene, pigeonholed into ghettos, corralled into its own schools, restricted to its own businesses, stigmatized and stunted—produced its own newspapers and magazines. It was done out of necessity. They did not come into being to celebrate the saintliness of black people. For black people were not, after all, noble savages, that is, children of nature mystically endowed with an overabundance of moral virtues. They did, in fact, lie, cheat and steal just like everyone else. But also—like everyone else—they were just a step below the angels. And so the black press came speaking of success as well as failure, of courage as well as cowardice. The black press came speaking not in stereotypes and shadows, but trying to illuminate the many nooks and crannies of the black community. The black press upheld the basic American concepts embodied in the Constitution and Declaration of Independence in its never-ceasing support and struggle for civil rights for all people, including black Americans.

Out of this historical tradition came *Ebony,* the publication with which I am most familiar. As has been the case with many of our predecessors in black journalism, *Ebony,* during its 25-year history, has been a vehicle for building and projecting a black image long since shattered and distorted by media oriented primarily to the dominant culture. It is significant that *Ebony,* which means "black," was started at a time when "black" was not a good word in the black community.

At the very beginning of our publishing venture, we wanted to correct the record. We wanted to counteract the crippling effects of a damaged and degraded self-image. We felt then — as we do now — that every man must have a wholesome image of himself before he can demand respect from others. Once his negative self-image had been correctly altered, the black American could, by his own new-found strength, force others to look upon him with greater sensitivity and realism. Indeed, others would see that black really can be beautiful.

Image building has not been *Ebony's* only role. Over the years we have discovered that it is not enough to reflect merely the brighter side of black life by highlighting black achievement. In our early days, we had measured achievement largely in material terms. Today, however, we also measure achievement with a host of other yardsticks, not the least of which is dedicated service to the cause of black liberation from disproportionate unemployment, substandard housing, inadequate education, and in general, black economic and political powerlessness. In other words, over the years *Ebony* has tried to change with the changing aspirations of the people it serves. Just as blacks have become more assertive in all areas of American life, so also has *Ebony* assumed a more aggressive posture.

Thus, our August 1965 special issue on "The White Problem in America" anticipated the Kerner Commission Report by three years. Our various historical series were forerunners of the present drive for more black history in school curricula. In short, our pages have meticulously documented the social revolution that is still unfolding in the nation.

But *Ebony's* concern has not been exclusively with racial conflict, for we believe the black community should be covered by journalists on a continuing basis and not just when it explodes. While it is true that a street demonstration generates excitement and therefore reader appeal, nevertheless it is a mistake for journalists to accord it more importance in the black community than, for example, a voter-education campaign. Indeed, if we may project from present political trends in the nation's major cities, intensive black participation in the electoral process may emerge as the big story of the seventies.

In other words, the quiet, less blatantly dramatic

events in the black community deserve attention. Reprints of a recent *Ebony* article instructing high school youngsters on how to ready themselves for college have been distributed widely. Our magazine has been a manual of information for blacks wanting to become businessmen. We also have published our share of articles on parties and cotillions, eligible bachelors and fashionable women to satisfy the varied tastes of our readers.

We try to reflect the black community back to itself. But I think we should not only do that. We should explain black people to black people. We have been doing that in our role of trying to build a better self-image—by running historical series, for example. Back in 1959 we gave one of our editors 14 months off to do research on a series of articles that resulted in a book called *Before the Mayflower: A History of the Black People* by Lerone Bennett. Mr. Bennett went on to become a very outstanding black historian as a result of that series.

I also think that we have to lead a little bit. However, publishers and publications can't be too far ahead of the readers. Then the reader does not envision these things that we write about as something within his power to accomplish. So we try to be ahead, but not too far ahead.

What I have just sketched, of course, does not exhaust *Ebony's* role as a communicator. For the explosive nature of race relations in this country obliges us not to seek refuge in the cult of objectivity, but to choose sides, that is, to serve as advocates for black people. Their limited gains in recent years have only served to remind us of how far so many of them have to go to gain economic, political and social parity. Blacks are still three times as likely to die in childbirth and infancy, three times as likely to be in poverty, and twice as likely to be jobless.

And so, by continuing to "stay on the case," as younger blacks would say, we in a sense keep our white counterparts honest. By and large, the daily newspapers are hidebound by their ancient tradition of reporting who, what, when, where and how, without seriously addressing themselves to the question—why?

For example, it is not enough for the press to dwell solely on the use of force and the takeover of campus buildings by black college students. Surely we are all justified in deploring such tactics. But, we are also obliged to determine just what it is that the students are trying, however crudely, to say to the nation. The gist of their thinking can be easily summarized. Essentially, they believe a sense of racial unity and purpose is absolutely necessary for the genuine emancipation of black people. They believe anything is to be encouraged that helps to build a sense of black unity, black history and culture, black awareness. They believe anything that detracts from this sense, anything that diverts or dilutes the attention of black people from their uniqueness, from their purpose, from their mystique, is a luxury that cannot be afforded at this critical juncture in history. Today's black students are in a race to build a sense of black unity, because they fear—rightly or wrongly—that a racial Armageddon will overtake them. This sense of urgency must be grasped if we in the communications industry are to understand the powerful forces motivating radical black students.

Whatever his efforts are at in-depth interpretations of campus rebellions, the black communicator's basic responsibility is to the black community. He must defend it against the distortions of white, so-called "experts" on black problems. For example, his black perspective should permit him to focus on the instability of the black family, as did the controversial Moynihan Report of a few years back. But his study should go further with the explanation of why this occurs in our society, and it should study the miracle of the black family's continued existence in the face of the overwhelming forces against its survival.

Even when a black communicator is employed by the general press, he must not lose his loyalty to the black community. This was beautifully demonstrated recently when reporter Earl Caldwell of *The New York Times'* San Francisco bureau refused to release his notebooks and tape-recorded interviews with Black Panthers. That is, he refused to turn these over to a grand jury investigation of the Black Panther Party. Through his lawyers, Caldwell quite rightly argued that by entering a grand jury room, he would ruin for all time the confidence of the black community in his integrity. Fellow black reporters who supported Caldwell's position with full-page ads in two New York newspapers, declared that they were not "the white world's spies in the black community" nor "undercover agents for federal, state or local law enforcement agencies."

Caldwell's case illustrates the heavy responsibilities of the black communicator to his black constituents. He must inform — certainly! He must inspire — to be sure! He must entertain—yes! But, above all, he must continue the historic tradition of black journalism. He must nurture a sense of mission about the black community, jealously guard its integrity and lovingly help it become what it can and must be—keeping in mind always Justice Holmes' words: "We must sail sometimes with the wind, sometimes against it; but we must sail and not drift or lie at anchor."

CHAPTER SIX

How Can the Federal Government Facilitate Communication within the City?

by
Benjamin F. Holman
Director, Community Relations Service
U. S. Department of Justice

MR. HOLMAN had a long and varied career in the news media before he became director of the Community Relations Service of the U. S. Department of Justice. He was producer of "News Four Probe," an NBC program on social issues in metropolitan Washington, and he was a reporter and commentator for the *Chicago Daily News,* Chicago's WBBM-TV, and CBS News. He has been active in several civil rights organizations, and was one of the founders of the Illinois Council for Freedom of Residence. His experience in communications media and civil rights work were excellent credentials for his post as director of a federal government agency that tries to deal with the problems of the inner city through direct action and with as few bureaucratic impediments as possible. Mr. Holman was a natural choice to discuss what the federal government could do to help the inner city.

HOW CAN THE FEDERAL GOVERNMENT FACILITATE COMMUNICATION WITHIN THE CITY?

The United States government, like racial minorities, is not a monolithic, homogeneous, think-alike establishment with its several million employees marching along in cadence, but rather a decentralized collection of individual agencies with as many approaches, viewpoints, interests, styles, and ambitions as one finds in the black Afro-American community or the brown Spanish-speaking community or the white community. And even when it comes to matters of communication in the inner city —which we know means with black people—it is quite apparent that the different agencies, depending upon the nature of their clients and the subjects with which they are concerned, have a variety of approaches and even various levels of interest in the subject.

I think that my own agency, the Community Relations Service of the Department of Justice, might be considered quite different from many others.

We are an organization designed to help local communities alleviate racial tensions. We do this by trying to get local communities to deal effectively with the problems and the difficulties of black and brown people. We are a non-litigative, non-investigatory agency; that is, we are not an FBI-type operation. We do not hand out money. We have no hard-line bureaucratic programs to administer. We really have only our power of persuasion to try to convince elements of the establishment to move positively toward dealing with the plight of oppressed minorities in the country. The fact that we have none of these traditional weapons of bureaucrats is in essence a strength and a source of our effectiveness. We do not get bogged down in the usual bureaucratic jungle that makes so many of our federal programs ineffective and inopportune when they attempt to deal effectively with the plight of the poor and minorities.

We consider ourselves free-swinging. I have no hesitation about calling anybody in Washington and telling them that whatever their intentions were their programs have gone astray and that these programs are not really helping the oppressed minorities that they were originally designed by the Congress to help. Our people have to deal with, and do not hesitate to deal with, governors and top business executives in the country and, in private at least, they speak very bluntly and directly to them. We do not hesitate to tell directors of most of the institutions in this country to give up their racist practices, because that is precisely what they are, and we try to get people to stop denying that this is the case.

Ours is a unique organization that deals across the board with any problem or any obstacle that is keeping minorities as third—fourth—or fifth-rate citizens in this country.

CRS is not a debate society. We try to make it an action-oriented organization. We set specific goals that we like to see effected in a community, such as improving ghetto schools or improving the relations between police and minorities. We work and try to develop strategy to effect this. We do not get into debates about administration policy as we are not charged with developing it, or deciding upon it, at least.

The biggest reinforcement for our efforts is the consequences of failing to take our advice. We get involved in problems at a time when the people within the establishment who have to deal with them down at the local level are at wits' end on how to deal with them. And, frankly, they welcome an outside force that can come in and view with a nonemotional perspective. That is really the major element of our effectiveness. However, we are not without wits of our own. Where there are examples of class discrimination or violation of the law, we are obviously in a position to refer the perpetrators to other elements in the government for appropriate action. There is an implied muscle there that often leads to our effectiveness.

Another thing — we really do not concern ourselves with the so-called black extremist groups. We are concerned about the plight of the *mainstream* of black America. We are concerned about the "silent minority" among black people who suffer daily and whom television and radio and newspapers largely ignore. The media are the ones that are concerned about the extremists; they are ones who feel that extremists make nice copy and pictures. The plight of the ordinary suffering black or brown persons apparently so far has not been considered very good copy for most of the media. They prefer to deal with the sensational extremists who are very much in the minority.

Recently, a newly-appointed executive in a federal agency, charged with improving the quality of life among our society's disadvantaged members, attempted to locate all the research that had been conducted into the news media habits and attitudes among poor people. He came to us for information because many of the disadvantaged—or whatever is the term currently in vogue to describe poor people—are also disadvantaged by skin color. We could only refer him to perhaps eight or ten pieces of research in this area, which is surprising when one considers that sociologists, psychologists, political scientists, and other students of human attitudes and behavior have been busily studying other aspects of the poor for the past ten years or so.

A cynic might say that this is so because the communication industry—newspapers, radio and television stations, networks, news services, magazines, and advertising and marketing specialists—don't really care what persons with low income and colored skins look at or listen to or read. Yet, when we see photos on television or in the newspapers and magazines on civil disturbances, inevitably the shots that the editors choose to bring to the public eye show some black kid running off with a television set. Or, when an editor chooses to withhold some scenes from the public, his rationale often is that using it would tend to stir up bad feelings among the "colored" folk.

During the past several years, the Community Relations Service has been involved in more than 30 conferences on the general subject of the news media and race relations. One of our major contributions to these conferences has been to suggest that the news media would be attracting larger minority audiences if they stopped depending upon one or two "Negro spokesmen" to tell them how it is. We have recommended that news media executives sit down in earnest and sincere, and sometimes heated, discussions with minority groups who can reflect the spectrum of thought, lifestyles, ambitions, interests, and problems. I believe that these conferences, and the various projects that have emanated from them involving both the news media and the community in constructive action, have made a significant contribution to racial progress in this country. Out of them have come training programs to put minority group members into careers in the news media, community-media committees that enable news executives and black and brown people to keep up an ongoing evaluation of the news media performance in regard to minorities, and in-service training on racial issues for members of news media staffs.

In March, 1969, the Urban Coalition issued a report on what progress had been made in the year after the National Advisory Commission on Civil Disorders issued what has come to be known as the Kerner Report. In that book—which probably is exceeded only by the Bible as the least-read best-seller in our history—the Kerner Commission leveled a number of charges against the media, including the statement that they largely report what happens through the white man's eyes. The Urban Coalition, in its report called "One Year Later," found that the news media were the only American institutions which showed some progress from 1968 to 1969 in handling racial issues—and unquestionably the Community Relations Service played a significant role in helping the news media to make that progress.

The news profession — or business — is still quite touchy when it comes to discussing its performance in regard to minority group members, especially if the criticism comes from government quarters. We still hear news executives make the defense that they only print or air what happens, serving as a mirror to the world. I think that it is not so much a mirror as a telescope that the news media hold to the world. What is called to our attention is that small chunk of our social landscape that someone in the news business who is master of the telescope chooses to focus on. Usually minorities suffer from what lens buffs call spherical aberration — fuzziness around the edges.

In the conferences in which we have been involved, it is common for black or brown people to complain to editors and news directors that the news media devote too much space and time covering bad news while ignoring the good news about minority group members. Marshall McLuhan, that often astonishing and sometimes outrageous critic of the media, recently commented on this subject of "bad news" that: "Ads are all good news, threatening daily changes to our way of life that would improve us beyond all recognition. Such persistent and innumerable threats to our continuitiy and integrity require quite a flood of bad news to make them bearable or saleable." Mr. McLuhan went on to observe that "We need only to open a trade journal — in which there is nothing but ads — to sense the importance of survivor emotion necessary to keep the audience afloat amidst the barrage of menacing promises." Whether or not one agrees with Mr. McLuhan, it is a fact that blacks and browns are particularly affected by the tendency of the news media to devote more attention to the bad news—crime, rape, and murder.

Not only does this policy tend to hammer down the hopes and ambitions of black and brown people, it tends to reinforce stereotypes about minority group members in the minds of whites.

It is for this very reason that I felt compelled to submit comments to the Federal Communications Commission last January on its proposed "Primer of Ascertainment of Community Problems." This primer dealt with the requirement that radio and television ascertain the "needs, taste and interests" of their audiences and that they make programs in response to their findings. The FCC proposed to make "needs, tastes and interests" synonymous with "community problems," which I felt would have compounded the objection that black and brown people continually are making—that the news media don't usually deal with minorities except in terms of violence.

Too much of the small amount of time devoted to the minority community is spent on violence and not enough on the other aspects of the lives of minority people—in-depth reporting on the underlying problems: hunger, overcrowding, poor schools, inadequate health services, high unemployment and underemployment rate, high crime rate, drug addiction, and high infant mortality rate. Furthermore, if the media are going to give these problems the proper attention, they must also concentrate on the white problem of institutional and individual racism, which is really the root cause of much of what prevails in the black and brown communities.

Because radio and television stations are licensed by the FCC, citizens have more opportunity to influence the practices and policies of the broadcast media than they do the print media.

The first radio station was licensed by the government nearly 50 years ago. In 1934, Congress passed the Communications Act, which stipulated that the airways were the public property, licensed to station operators upon the fulfillment of certain conditions. Over the years, the FCC has established regulations to serve as guides in issuing new licenses or renewing existing ones every three years.

A citizen or organization has had the potential for affecting station policies and operations since 1934, but it has only been in the last few years that the power of citizen action has been recognized. Those anti-smoking commercials you see on television are the result of a young man's determination to get the FCC to declare that the so-called Fairness Doctrine ought to be applied in allowing the other side of the story to be presented in answering the claims of sponsored cigarette commercials.

Black groups in some communities have asked that the FCC apply the Fairness Doctrine to their interests and require stations to present both sides of such controversial issues as civil rights and racial integration. In June, 1969, the FCC ordered radio and television stations to eliminate discrimination in every aspect of station employment policies and practices. Limited successes of minority community groups on employment and programming have encouraged challenges to station license renewals or ownership transfers in a number of communities in recent years.

In Jackson, Mississippi, a black and white group, supported by the United Church of Christ, challenged the renewal of WLBT-TV on charges of racially biased programming. The FCC, in 1966, barred the petitioners from the renewal proceedings, but the courts, in 1969, granted the petitioners' demand for withdrawal of WLBT's license. It is likely that other stations have been more willing to consider the demands of minority groups since that decision.

However, challenging a license renewal through the FCC or the courts is an expensive, time-consuming process, and most minority groups realistically hope only to influence stations to change their practices and policies in accordance with FCC regulations.

An integrated group in Texarkana, Arkansas, in 1969, sought to reduce discrimination at KTAL-TV through the device of negotiation with the station. A list of demands concerning programming and employment practices was submitted by the group, and the FCC renewed the license of KTAL-TV contingent upon the signing of a contract between the station and the citizen's group to enforce the demands. The FCC stated that the owners would continue to hold their license based upon their performance on the contract.

In February, 1970, 18 groups in Atlanta, Georgia, formed the Community Coalition in Broadcasting, a predominantly black group, to use the Texarkana contract model to negotiate with the owners of the 28 radio and television stations operating in the Atlanta area. Ten teams of citizens, assisted by the United Church of Christ and the Citizens Communication Center of Washington, began negotiating with the station owners in an attempt to get them to sign a contract with the Coalition covering all stations. Significant results have been accomplished, including a concerted effort by one station to interview blacks in various positions, assignment of a black as anchorman on a television news broadcast, coverage of black news events by integrated news crews, and the indication by at least five stations that they are willing to sign the contract.

Radio and television played a dramatic role in bringing the struggles of the civil rights movement for equality, especially in the South, into the eyes and ears of all Americans. Yet, strangely enough, few stations have gone beyond the obvious and vicious aspects of racism by making significant changes in their own policies and programming to deal with the more sophisticated, subtle forms of white racism that deprive black and brown people all over this nation.

The Community Relations Service helps minority groups call these deficiencies to the attention of the news media. We suggest ways we think that media performance in regard to minorities could be improved, and constantly remind them of the recommendations in Chapter 15 of the Kerner Report.

But vast improvement is still needed, not only for minorities but also for the benefit of the majority who really suffer most from this news diet deficiency.

It is perhaps remarkable that the news media, in these days of violence that involve persons of all races, are still being accorded by the civil rights movement the same approach used over the past decade. There have been few picket lines or bombings of broadcast stations or newspapers by dissident groups.

Our experience in communities indicates that black and brown people, at least for the present, prefer sitting down with media executives and employing the techniques of negotiation to resolve the difficulties. The media cannot afford not to respond in kind.

CHAPTER SEVEN

Can the Disadvantaged in the Inner City Learn to Communicate?

by
Budd Schulberg
Author, Founder of
Watts Writers Workshop

MR. SCHULBERG is an internationally famous writer who cared enough to make an individual effort to help the people of the inner city. On his own, he started the Watts Writers Workshop to try to help the talented people of the inner city develop their talents, which might otherwise be forever lost. Mr. Schulberg taught in the workshop alone for many months. He still tries to do some teaching but the operation has become so large and successful that administration and fundraising now occupy most of his time. His own credits include novels and screenplays, of which the best-known efforts have been *Sanctuary V* (1970), the screenplays for *On the Waterfront* and *A Face in the Crowd*, plus *The Harder They Fall* (1947), and *What Makes Sammy Run* (1941). Because of his teaching experience in Watts, Mr. Schulberg was assigned the topic "Can the Disadvantaged in the Inner City Learn to Communicate?" However, as he made clear in his lecture, he feels very strongly that the question should be turned around and that the problem really is "Can the Outside, Advantaged Society Learn to Communicate with the Disadvantaged in the Inner City?"

Back in 1965 I watched the rioting in Watts on television. It was an incredible sight. It was one of those times when television as a medium seemed to come into its own. We put TV down a lot—all those bad series and shows—but, every once in a while, you do get kind of a jolt, and you are able to see something like what was happening in Watts. Something like that comes along and you feel that television can bring some living experience right into your lap. That was what I felt as I watched South Los Angeles going up in flames—people burning their own buildings, their own streets and their own houses.

It happened that an Eastern columnist was there with me. He thought that I knew about this, since I had been brought up in Los Angeles and had gone to school there—Los Angeles High School and all of that—and he asked me what was happening.

Well, beyond knowing that some terrible human explosion was going on, I did not really know. I could speak in generalities. I felt a little embarrassed that I did not know more. I had been raised in the tradition of the novel, and, ever since Mark Twain, Frank Norris, and through many people—Upton Sinclair, Jack London, and on up to Steinbeck, etc. — I think it has been expected of writers to be more than just novelists, more than just entertainers, that they ought to know what is going on, especially in their own neck of the woods.

And, though I had been asked a number of times

how the Watts thing got going, I did not really know. I just knew that as I watched, I became very eager to go to Watts.

So, on the first day of the curfew-lifting, about 72 hours after that question from the columnist, I simply drove there.

I got out in about the center of Watts. The fires were out, but it was still smoking. Many of the empty lots— they were now empty — reminded me of a mouth with most of its teeth knocked out. You would see a building here and there—one or two on a block and then everything between flat or, I should say, rubble, smoldering and smoking.

I went to the only place I could find where I might get some answers — a place called Westminster. It was sort of an old settlement house at that time, and there were about six or seven people on the staff. It was very run-down. It was the only thing in the block that was not burned down.

And I went in and just said what I had come for. I was taken around by a young lady from City College of New York. She was working there, and she said she would walk me around. She walked me through the streets and over to Jordan Downs, a housing project, and I began to get some sense of what was missing.

She rattled off figures to me, but they did not mean as much to me that day as they did later. The dropout rate, by the time a class in the junior high school got through the high school, was about 90 per cent. About a third of everybody was unemployed. For young people from 18 to 25, unemployment went as high as 75 per cent. And you could see them on the street, in the lots, in the pool rooms.

I felt this terrible, frightening hatred. People would shout out at me as I walked down the street.

I went into a pool room. There were about eight or ten young people in the pool room, and I was introduced. Nobody would shake my hand. they just looked up and down the wall. But I stayed there. They had a beat-up television set there. I sat in the back and I watched it as the pool game went on — they were very good pool shooters, by the way — and I got my first little flicker of education.

The television shows, especially the commercials, made me very uncomfortable. They were showing all the things—the houses and other things—that these people, ragged and pretty beat, would obviously never have. It finally got to a commercial about how you could have your own home, only so much down, right on the golf course, every house opening out on the golf course with a swimming pool, etc., and they started to laugh. One of them said, "I'm going to have two." They were funny, but I do not think I have ever looked at commercials in the same way again after coming from that pool hall.

At the end of the day, I came back to this place called Westminster, feeling discouraged and understanding why people might light fires. Seeing that the fires had been selective, I kept asking, "Why is that burned?" And they said, "Well, that was, you know, a pawn shop and they were gouging." And I would say, "Why wasn't that burned?" and they would say that that was something else. They felt that the places they had spared were doing some good. I had not thought of a riot or fires of that kind being selective.

I asked if there was anything I could do. I said, "You know, I am not the NAACP and I am not the Job Corps. I don't come from the government. Is there anything one person can do?"

And this young lady rather angrily said, "Well, you may think these young kids on the corner and these kids dropping out and these kids in the pool rooms and any one of the kids setting the fires, you may think that they are idiots, that they are stupid. We've run some tests. Some of them are amazing. Some of them have high I.Q.'s and still they haven't gone through the 10th grade. Some of them could be something — there go nuclear physicists, there go writers; God knows what they could become, but look at them. They aren't going to be anything. They are going down."

So I got the idea of starting this writing class, and I put it up on the bulletin board of this organization. I just simply said, "Creative writing class, all interested sign below." I said I would be back every Friday afternoon.

I came back the next Friday. Nobody had signed up,

but there were a couple of suggestions on the sheet for me. And I came back again and again—I was in a small pantry off a kitchen room—and I waited. Nobody came. And this went on for about six weeks.

I learned more about Watts because I talked to some of the people working there — some of the staff would drop in. Some of them felt sorry for me, and I would read the throwaway sheets and the papers and things like that. At least I was getting an education. But I was almost ready to give up. I thought I would give it until about the end of December, and this was now October.

I was reading a lot. I took *Man Child in the Promised Land* down there and I read the autobiography of Malcolm X and some stuff by Kenneth Clark. I was sort of preparing myself for this class—this nonexistent class.

And then, finally, just before I thought I would pack the whole thing up, a fellow called Charles showed up. I had seen him; I had met him in the pool room. He asked me what this was. He said he had gone to a year or two of high school and he had had a pretty rough time. He had been in the riot, which, by the way, they never called a "riot." They always referred to it as the "revolt." And the first time I said "riot," they said, "What riot, man? You're talking about the revolt."

So he had been in the revolt and had been in jail about two weeks. He showed me some of the scars, and he said, "What is this? I don't understand what it's all about." So I told him it was a writing class, and I read to him out loud about a page of Claude Brown. It was a page on which Claude, when he is a young kid—I think he was 11 years old—has missed a day or two of a riot and of the pillaging. He has been sick or something, and he cannot make it. "You can go into these places, the windows are broken, you can walk right in and take anything you want." And Claude, in the book, says, "Man, when are we going to have another one?"

And when I read that, Charles said, "Gee, I didn't know you could write that in a book." It had some four-letter words, but it was not so much the four-letter words, it was that someone could say exactly what they were doing—put it down as it was and, in a sense, confess it or explain it, and not get arrested for it. He was amazed.

And he said—and this was kind of a breakthrough —he said, "Is that writing?"

And I said, "This is a big successful book. This is a best seller. It is not only on *The New York Times* best seller list, but it is number one. This is a book that people are reading all over the country."

And he said, "You know, if you can write that, I can write lots of stuff like that."

And I said, "Well, good, start."

And the next time he came, he brought a couple of fellows from the pool room, and this was the nucleus of our class.

He told me, after I got a little friendly with him, "Now I'm going to tell you the truth. When you came down to rap on the corner, we were saying, 'Who was that grey cat? He can't be up to any good.'" And they had wanted to stomp me. And some goodness in Charles reached out and he said, "Well, let me try to find where he's at first." Apparently it was that curiousity about me at the beginning rather than any real interest in creative writing that brought Charles in there.

But he finally got in and started. And, once he got in, he did become awfully interested in trying to put down what had happened to him and where he went, and he became sort of a missionary for the class and brought in others.

By the winter of 1966 we had a class of about seven or eight, and they were a very mixed bag. Four or five were 18 or 19 and two or three were in their 40's, those in their 40's having had less education than the younger ones. They had gone through three, four, or five grades; some of the younger ones had gone through nine, ten, or eleven, but I saw as I looked at their work that the formal education did not really matter; it did not matter what grade they had been in.

One youngster who had dropped out of the 10th grade—his name was Sammy Harris—was a young man of the streets who had been hungry for a long time and who was living in the backs of cars. He had a very small record, for things like loitering.

He showed me a poem. I looked at the title and I looked at him. The title was "Infinite." And it started off — I cannot repeat it from memory, unfortunately —

something like: "Never know a begin of me, Lord God gave to me."

My first impulse was to say, "Well, 'begin' isn't the word. You know, it's 'beginning.'" But then, the more I looked at this poem which was semi-literate, the more it struck me that this was a pretty damn original poem. It said, "For life is origin, process, change causing origin, process, change," and it went on for about eight lines, "origin, process, change" going slanting right off the paper.

I asked him about his poetry, and where he got it from. He said he just liked to do it. He showed me these sketches, and said he liked to write poetry. He said that if I would like to see more he would bring a poem the next week.

The next week he brought in one that I thought was also remarkable. It was called, "One, Two, Three." In some way it was about the Trinity.

In a sense, what we had was a young poet on our hands who had never been reached in school. I asked him if the English teacher had ever talked to him about his poetry, and he said, "The English teacher didn't know I write poetry." And I asked him if he had read much, because some of his poetry sounded like William Blake to me. I was not sure that he had not cribbed a little from Blake. And he said, "Blake who?" I tried to get him to read Blake; later he did, but not with great success. At other times, he sounded like Rimbaud, but he had not known of any of these people.

There were others like Sammy Harris. There was a

fellow, James Thomas Jackson, who I felt wrote pretty well. He said he was working on a novel. I looked at a piece of it. It was a good chapter of a novel. It was well done.

I asked James about his writing. He said that he came from Houston and had hitch-hiked in on the first night of the fires in Watts. He did not know what was going on. He was just stopped by the cops and dragged in, and the next thing he knew he was in jail, and he did not even know what the trouble was in Los Angeles.

He said he had some more chapters. I said I would like to read them. He said he worked at night as a janitor in a bar. And so, a couple of nights after that, I stopped in. It was as low a crumby type of bar as you can find. James Thomas Jackson was sweeping out the bar as it was about to close. He was being paid two dollars a night and all the beer he could drink. I must say this for James Thomas Jackson; he was not only a pretty good writer, but like many writers, he could drink quite a lot of beer. And again, as with Sammy and maybe five or six others I have now become pretty well acquainted with, I was struck by the contrast between where he was in this bar practically skid-rowish—and what he seemed able to do.

The others were much the same. There was a woman called Birdell Chew who had been a domestic. She had always wanted to write. I looked at her work, and my first reaction was "forget it." I felt that I had found some people with unique talent, like Sam Harris, and there were others like Emmery Evans and Vallejo Ryan Kennedy, all who had dropped out of school, but all with a kind of fresh approach. But when I looked at Birdell Chew's work, it just looked hopeless. It was usually without punctuation, and if there was punctuation it was completely arbitrary. There would be semicolons for no reason. It did not begin or end. It was mostly all in present tense. The syntax was completely out of whack. It was so bad that I put it aside as hopeless.

One Sunday when I had some extra time, I started to put things into different piles, which led later to the anthology that we published called *From the Ashes*. I took Birdell's story out. Then I picked it up again, and thought I would give it a chance. This time I read it with a pencil in my hand, and I did very simple things to it. I corrected spelling, put in a period every so often, and made capitals at the beginnings of sentences. And then I had it typed up and I read it, and it became like a picture that is completely out of focus and somehow comes into sharp focus.

The story was about two little children, very small, four or five years old, in the swamps of Louisiana. The dialogue was strange to me. They did not use "I," for instance. They used "me hungry, me do this," etc. And they were described by Birdell as living like little animals. Their parents went off in the fields and they just kind of lived. No one really took care of them. They did not go to school. They played in the swamp every day together.

One day, they go further into the swamp. They just get carried away. They are following a bird—I think it was a bluebird—and they follow it along, as children will, and they get further and further out until finally they are at the other end of the swamp. They come out onto sort of a grassy plateau, and they see a house, a little house, and it is extremely pretty. It is painted white. It has a nice pretty cloth on top of a pole. And then they see a whole bunch of children—15 or 20—come out, and they see a woman who does not look old enough to have that many kids and they cannot understand what this place is. They spy on it day after day, and they do not understand what they have found. Of course, the reader knows what they have found is a school. Finally, they are discovered and dragged in—terrified like trapped animals—dragged right into the school and they find out what it is. After that they want to go there, but over the objections of their parents who are afraid of the master and feel that this is just going to cause trouble.

By this time our class had become pretty big. There were about 20 in it now. We read the story out loud, and people really cried at the story. It gave Birdell a new kind of feeling. In fact, she said, "I have been saying to people that I am a writer for 20 years, and everybody has always laughed at me, because they say 'You can't even spell your name.'"

In the summer of 1966, one year after that, we did a television show as part of the Watts Summer Festival.

It was put on NBC. It was a fairly simple plan—just writers in the workshop, as we were doing it then, reading their works. They would read their work and the camera would just swing out over Watts and more or less show—try to reflect or symbolize—what they were writing about. And the thing did well; it caused a sensation. We had, according to NBC, the heaviest mail on a show of that kind that they had ever had. Letters came in asking about Sammy Harris—saying he reminded people of Blake; saying that Johnie Scott, who was born and raised in Watts and who was 19 years old at that time, was possibly a genius.

By that time, we had grown out of the pantry—more people were coming in. We took a little house — it had been completely wrecked—on Beach Street. All the windows were knocked in; it was a mess. We fixed it up and we made it the center for the Watts Writers' Workshop. We talked about a name for it, and somehow we fell on the idea of naming it for Frederick Douglass, since Douglass had been a slave who had escaped to the North and had become a famous abolitionist, both as an orator and a writer. He had written a book which in its day was enormously influential in bringing to the people of the North what it was to be a slave. It was called *My Bondage and My Freedom.* And so we named the house Douglass House.

By that time, people were just walking in off the street. Youngsters would come in and say, "Is this where you read the poetry?"

And someone else would say, "Yeah."

And they would say, "Well, I've got a poem here." It began to seem at times as if everybody in Watts was a writer.

By this time we had 10 or 12 able poets. I said then —as I lived in Beverly Hills uptown—that, "God almighty, I would match our poets against any damn poets in Southern California. They would absolutely wipe out Beverly Hills High School." I have seen the Beverly Hills High School literary magazine, and it is very thin. And our stuff stood out.

We had started to publish first in a magazine called *Los Angeles,* and then *Scholastic* magazine, which goes to all English classes in public high schools across the country, published excerpts from our poets. Here was, in a sense, the phenomenon of youngsters publishing in a high school newspaper like *Scholastic* who themselves were not able to make it in or through the high school. I began to wonder, to generalize about this.

We kept on, by the way, growing all the time, to about 40 or 50, and we finally moved on to the main street. "Charcoal Alley No. 1" it was called because that was where the main fires were. It was 103rd Street. We took over a burned-out supermarket to accommodate the larger classes. We also set it up, at that time, as a very crude theater. Some of those who were in the classes tried writing plays, and when they had a play, naturally they wanted to try to get the play on. So we started to put plays on, and some of the people in the class became interested in acting through that.

A great many of these people were people not only without education but, to some extent homeless and greatly troubled. I had not anticipated—just out of my own ignorance—that you could not separate the work of these young poets or playwrights from the daily travail of their lives and, although I had read about it, I had not really realized the intense pressure of the society—of the police—on these people. I found there that there was truly a constant harassment, and that we were spending a good deal of our time getting members of the workshop out of jail, almost as much as were trying to get their works published or trying to get their plays on the stage. At the same time, we built up a kind of esprit de corps through that. I think I simply began to feel that this was not just another white "do-good" effort; that the people would stand with their classmates and would fight for them as well as try to create with them.

A couple of years ago—by this time we were considered successful—we had published our book, quite a few of the people were publishing on their own, and we had set up national tours, possibly for the first time out of the black ghetto, in which six or eight young poets would tour campuses. We were considered successful, but I considered it just a bare start. We were asked to come to Washington, three or four members of the workshop and myself, to testify for Senator Ribicoff's committee which was looking into urban problems, urban disorder, and the rest of it.

What I tried to say in that Senate hearing was that I thought I had stumbled almost accidentally on pools of talent that I had not expected. I really had not expected anything like the success we have had. By this time, we had started to duplicate it, and to set up other centers, smaller ones in Long Beach and San Bernadino, and a Mexican one in the East Los Angeles section, and in Altadena, Pasadena, and San Francisco. They were starting to function pretty well.

I suggested at that hearing that if we had tapped oil, you would have heard a scream from that Senate. You would have heard a shout from the business community. If this were oil coming down from Alaska they would be saying, "Let's not lose it. Let's put up the money to bring up the pipe. Let's do this and that." But when it is talent, when it is people, when it is art, and, possibly, when it is black, then there is not the same kind of excitement and there is not the same kind of support. For the lack of that sort of tapping, or building ways out and putting those pipes in, there is going to be in the ghetto talent wasted —just pouring off like oil into the ground—going deeper and deeper, wasted, and at the same time, a growing bitterness.

That bitterness I still feel in Watts despite what we have done. And we have now built a modern full-fledged theater there that can show films, which they did not have before. But, despite a little thing here and a little thing there, there is bitterness and anger growing because of a lack of concern.

The question asked here, "Can the Disadvantaged in the Inner City Learn to Communicate?" is to me not exactly the question. The question to me is—about these people who are neglected, and I could use a much stronger word, in the ghetto; about they who obviously can communicate, can communicate with each other, and can communicate to other people brilliantly—"Can the Outside, Advantaged Society Learn to Communicate *with Them?*"

That is the bridge I think has to be built. But it is one minute to midnight. I am not at all confident that we can.

CHAPTER EIGHT

How Can the People's Voice Be Heard in the Inner City?

by
Royce Hanson
President
Washington Center for Metropolitan Studies

DR. HANSON has an impressive record in research, education, publication, and public service. He is president of the Washington Center for Metropolitan Studies and is a professor in the School of Government and Public Administration at American University. He has twice run for the House of Representatives from his district in Maryland, and has been a delegate to the Maryland Constitutional Convention and the Democratic National Convention. He has been a consultant on various public bodies on the local, county, state, and national levels. Dr. Hanson has lectured and written widely on urban affairs, political parties, state government, and American political thought. Because of the nature of his achievements and the work of the Center he was in an ideal position to speak on how people in the inner city could make their voices heard.

HOW CAN THE PEOPLE'S VOICE BE HEARD IN THE INNER CITY?

I was very intrigued by this question, "How Can the People's Voice Be Heard in the Inner City?"

But who are the people? What is their voice? What is it saying? To whom is it saying whatever it is saying? Through which media does that voice speak and, especially, to what effect?

We tend to be the victims of our own stereotypes about people and about the people in and of the inner city. I suspect that this question, properly analyzed, means "How can the voices of the people in the inner city be heard?"

But what kinds of voices are we talking about? The voices of the militant? the alienated? the young? the elderly? the law-abiding? the criminal? the victim of crime? the ex-convict? the home owner? the shopkeeper? the merchant? the union member? the block organizer? the exploited? the exploiter? the addict? the pusher? the minister? the dude? the worker? the unemployed?

For all of these are parts of the inner city. In fact, contrary to our stereotyped notion of the inner city, I think we would find far more variety among the interests that exist within the inner city and the potential voices that might be heard there than we would find in any other part of the metropolitan area. But we often imagine it to be of one character. I do not know why, but we seem to expect one voice from the inner city.

All that said, the question keeps coming back in any kind of program or project that deals with the inner city:

"But who are the leaders? No, no, I don't mean *those;* I mean who are the *real* leaders of the inner city?" I am both dismayed and a little amused that we tend to reject as leaders those who do not fit our own images of typicality or authenticity. We are all for the maximum feasible participation of those who "ought to" maximally, feasibly participate. We look for legitimacy and we tend to confer legitimacy on those whom we designate as leaders. The politics of leadership in this situation tends often to be inverted, in that the external audiences often precede the development of an internal constituency. And when the audience gets tired, then the constituency that has been created on the basis of having an external audience may also tend to diminish or evaporate.

These things are, I think, only superficial manifestations of the problem, which is the seeming lack of inner city publics that can command attention and sustain action. And this brings me to examine the nature of public opinion in an urban society and the crucial relationship that most of us would concede exists between our system of communication and the existence and health of a polity in the inner city.

Here I propose to use a definition of public opinion that some of my friends who are not, as I am, disciples of Machiavelli might find offensive. This definition of public opinion goes as follows: Public opinion is that opinion which officials find it prudent to heed.

Now, if the voices we hear, that is, if the public

opinions of the people of the inner city are not heeded, *why not?* And what is required to change those circumstances? Here we return to the question of who the publics are and the very nature of publics. I think for a good understanding of this particular problem we need to think about that a bit. For a public to function there must be officials. There can be no public without officials and without officials who are in some way dependent upon that public. When an issue is no longer private but has become a matter of shared experience of two or more people, for them to *deal* with that question requires the existence of a public official. That public official may be a citizen; he may also be an elected person or a bureaucrat, but an official is required. Most cities are not structured to give an ear to a geographically isolated public. The structure of our official system is such that it is far more convenient for publics to organize by functional interests rather than by geographic locations. This is, in part, the nature of the modern city and the modern world. This has been made so by the development of communication and transportation technology.

However, a great deal of our imagery of public life —in Lippmann's phrase, "the pictures in our heads"— is based on a society and a social order that has not existed since about 1910. Think of where your friends live and where the other members of the publics of which you are a member live and ask yourself how many of these can be described as neighborhood publics or communities in a geographic sense of that term. The more diverse the functional interests that exist within a geographic area—and I have already suggested that an inner city may have more diverse interests within it than any other part of the metropolis — the more difficult is the organization of an area base public, all the rhetoric expended upon the term community to the contrary notwithstanding.

One reason for functional organization is that it is on that basis that interests and experience are most often shared on subjects such as education, employment opportunities, wages and salaries, transportation or housing. There may be geographic aspects to some of these problems but they are certainly not confined to any specific geographic area nor are the people with whom one, even in the inner city, shares experiences and attitudes.

Government is also better organized to deal with problems than with areas. Most of our governmental departments on state, federal and local levels are organized by someone's perception of a problem at some period of time. And most were organized to deal with perceptions of problems that existed some time ago, as contrasted with today's perceptions of problems. And, further, people tend to view problems in light of the way in which they are organized to view problems.

Now, what I am leading up to is the point that shared experience on problems or functions makes possible the development of political coalitions. And when the voices of the people of the inner city are heard and heeded it is very often because their experiences and interests are shared by others. I think we have had one very good example of this in the District of Columbia in recent years, and this has been the organization of the Emergency Committee on the Transportation Crisis.

Was this organization an expression of the voice of the inner city? It was initially organized by people who did *not* live in the inner city. As the transportation interests of some people in the inner city began to be felt and expressed, inner-city people, or some inner-city people, began to take substantial roles in the leadership of the committee. The point is that it appears to have expressed a substantial public interest felt by a substantial public in that part of the city. It also expressed interests of others in other parts of the city, and it did exercise influence. Other examples might involve other groups whose interests might be quite diverse on a broad range of things, but which coalesce on only one problem or a very narrow range of problems.

The inner city is often not heard when it has no external allies, as in the early days of urban renewal, and when there is no point of access in the political system—no official, if you please, who is dependent on a public and who also has the power or potential power to exercise a veto, either legally or practically, and therefore must be negotiated with in order to obtain an agreement. The who, the publics, have to be assembled in a manner that makes it possible for them to be heard. Otherwise, the inner city remains a private and not a public concern. Now, what is said by the inner city is also often said in functional terms, but there is no one clear message. That really should be expected where there are many existing and potential publics as a result of forming a comprehensive public for the inner city, or as a result of the difficulty of forming a comprehensive public for the inner city as such, and the corollary insensitivity of our public processes. It is not unusual at all, it seems to me, that there is not one voice. I would argue that the demand which often may be made—and I think it is quite frankly an open political demand—to people of the inner city is, "Why we would be glad to listen to you if you would get yourselves together."

Having participated in suburban politics, I know of nothing more disorganized than the voice of the suburbs. We should not really expect that the suburbs would speak as one voice. But we have so overcome our own impressions of the suburbs that our stereotypes carry us through all the disharmonies that are apparent all around us, and so we tend to speak of the interests of the suburbs as if they were one easily defined thing and the interests of the inner city as if they were one easily defined thing. We then find it easy to say that urban problems are the central city — or the inner city — against the suburbs and that these two are in conflict. If one looks closely at the character of the population of the metropolitan area, and at the political interests of people in various parts of that area, he finds that some suburbanites are really living downtown. If the stereotyped attitude describes what they do and how they feel, some of them live in the black ghettos. He also finds that some inner-city types are really living in the suburbs.

Tactics as well as content are a part of the public message. They are a part of what is said. Form may be as important as substance if McLuhan has even a germ of validity to him. Both are integral to the message. Those who would form publics — when isolated from others who could share their experience, whom they cannot seem to reach — tend toward extreme tactics as well as extreme statements.

A problem of urban politics, particularly where apathy abounds, is to convert insensitivity of feeling into mass support. The means of doing this are pretty important. Confrontation may be only a tactic but it may also be the substance of the message that gets through to the auditor. Extreme or violent behavior may attract support and may help build a public. It may also further alienate potential support, both in and out of the immediate audience. The behavior may be more important ultimately than the content or the subject matter about which that behavior is directed in its public effect and response — which brings me to the media.

The media are essential to the development of any public. How does one otherwise obtain and sustain communication on major issues? The mass media are essential, especially when the ordinary representative processes tend not to be able to respond very well to new stimuli.

Now the inadequacies of the media are legend and scholars such as Spiro Agnew have documented this in substantial detail.

They are susceptible to manipulation by those who like to manipulate them and have an interest in so doing. Because of the way in which they work they tend to incite those who would be newsworthy to do newsworthy things that will attract and retain the attention of the media. Retaining this interest, I think, is where we get into trouble, because one has to keep raising the ante a little bit in order to get the media to come back to cover the next outburst. The newspapers, after all, are not the only people—nor are the television stations—who have news sense about them. Quite frequently in my own political campaigns—and I know this is not unique to me—I would sit around with my staff in the morning and the opening question was, "What can we do to get in the papers?"

There is also the problem of selectivity in what is covered, but I think that probably more important are the economics of the media, which tend, first of all, to favor international and national news over local news. One of the reasons for this is that it is cheaper per unit to cover international and national news. It can be done through newspaper pools and wire services with far more complete coverage of what is happening in Washington, Paris, the United Nations and so on, than through providing comparably competent and insightful coverage of what is happening in the local community. Communications builds it own audience that expects certain kinds of coverage and is not interested in other sorts of coverage, and I think that the economics are a reinforcing element.

The space problem, whether it is air space or newspaper space, tends also to favor dramatic conflict as a most economic way of attracting mass audiences, and the most attractive way of expanding the realm of the conflict, because the basic strategy of the underdog is to yell for help. If one is winning the battle, one does not particularly covet newspaper coverage of that event because it could excite someone. On the other hand, if one is on the losing end of a battle, there is a need to expand the arena to get more people involved, to find out if there is not someone who is standing around watching who will quit watching and jump in on the side of the underdog.

Perhaps even more important than the problems of the media is the problem of institutional access both through the media and through political organizations in the government. Where there are representatives and officials who represent, publics can be created. We often expect that the voice of the inner city will emerge from the grass roots, full blown and strident and informed and ready to take its full place in the public arena. We assume the same thing for rural poverty areas or any other group that is generally excluded. However, we know that that is not the way public opinion is organized and publics are formed. But, as Lippmann perceived long ago, they are very often formed by opinion leaders who assert a point of view and then go out and organize people and their ideas to support that point of view.

Where, for instance, did the opposition to Judge G. Harrold Carswell come from? Did it come full-blown from the grass roots of America? Were there millions and millions of Americans sitting around cogitating over this momentous public decision that had to be made and simultaneously coming to the conclusion that this man was not quite up to the standard that ought to be required of a justice of the Supreme Court—without the slightest amount of prompting from Senator Birch Bayh or the AFL-CIO or Joseph Rauh or Roy Wilkins or anyone else? I rather doubt that.

When such institutions for the formation of opinion are lacking, the politics of accommodation then fail, because some are excluded from the arena and ignored in the resulting political compromises that are made. We are confronted, then, with weaknesses in our political system, our political institutions, and in our administrative system which often—not with initial intent but with the practical result—overlook potential publics and make it extremely difficult for those publics to become *actual* in their operation and for them to have officials with whom to interact.

This causes, in turn, the emergence of the old legitimacy question and the problem of who can really speak for the inner-city interests. (It is curious to me that we never wonder who can really speak for the suburbanite.)

What effect does all this have? What effect does the voice of the inner city have?

Well, I am reminded of a story told me once by a judge who spent 20 years as an assistant solicitor general of the United States and who tried many cases before the Supreme Court. He tells of a lawyer from Nebraska who was trying his first case before the supreme Court, a very important tax case. They started argument on Friday and he had only got through his opening paragraphs when the time for argument on that day ended. Chief Justice Fred Vinson asked him if he would be willing to come back Monday to conclude his argument, which, of course, he was. Over the weekend, someone took him sailing on the Chesapeake Bay and he caught cold, developed laryngitis, and could hardly speak when the court resumed on Monday.

Having never tried cases before the Supreme Court before, he was trying to show how knowledgeable he was of the intricacies of the tax law, and he was never getting to the point of whether or not what had been done was unconstitutional. He interrupted himself every now and then and said, "Mr. Chief Justice, this is a very important point and I hope the court *understands* what I have to say." And he would go on with more of this argument and again stop and say, "Mr. Chief Justice, I hope the court understands me because this *is* very important."

After he had done this several times the Chief Justice interrupted him and said, "Counsel, the court *hears* you."

Now, very often the voice of the inner city is heard and not understood. Is the hearing of that voice productive or counterproductive? Is it heard but not heeded? For ultimately what we are interested in, in the development of public opinion, is having opinion heeded.

We may hear the riots. But we may not understand them, and if the message is not understood, then the action that is likely to be taken is probably not going to ameliorate the problem or respond to the problem that exists. Palliatives are often applied, in the way of saying "We hear you. Why don't you be quiet and we'll do something. Go away. Don't bother us anymore because, after all, we've done something."

But I think that what we are after is some kind of sustained effort based on a continuing understanding, a shared interest in the sorts of problems we imagine that the inner city has and which people in the inner city *feel* that they have. The answer to the question originally posed, then, involves more than the usual amount of breast-beating and guilt-motivated approaches like hiring more black reporters and having more inner-city coverage and doing a special here and there on a particular problem, which may help. It may be nice, but it may also only fuel the stereotypes.

I think that some of the most useless endeavors I have been engaged in have been things like being on a committee to go listen to people tell us about their problems. I think this is counterproductive for those who are doing the listening and especially for those who are doing the talking, because generally those listening are not officials and have no ability to act. So they do not act. And when they do not, the reaction of a person trying to do the communicating in the first place is, "What good does it do to communicate in that particular way?"

I am inclined to think that what is really required is the opportunity for more experience in democracy through the restructuring and reforming of political institutions. Communicating about some of these problems may do more, ultimately, to assist the voice of the inner city to be heard than certain, short-range, palliative, "nice" things do. We need to expand the opportunity for political experience and this will ultimately, it seems to me, call on us to seriously restructure our representative system, the kind of issue on which no public attention is ever focused.

We need to restructure our administrative system so that publics can be organized, so that legitimate spokesmen can be developed, so that leaders can gain experience, so that a broader range of people can participate in public affairs, and so that the hearing of the myriad voices of the inner city becomes a natural course of a political process, not something that we induce in a special Sunday edition of the paper or in a special listening post committee or in a set of public hearings. All those things may be needed, but I would suggest that they are not fundamental to resolution of the question.

Thus, while I am not offering anything very specific, I am suggesting that hearing is quite an incomplete part of the process and that to *understand* we will have to have a far more sophisticated use of the media—not just the communications media but the other media of political communication, the representative processes, and the structure of government—than we have developed in our cities up to this time.

CHAPTER NINE

The Future of Communication in Megalopolis

by
Wolf Von Eckardt
Architecture Critic
The *Washington Post*

THE FUTURE OF COMMUNICATION IN MEGALOPOLIS

MR. VON ECKARDT has written widely for magazines on city planning, architecture, and design. His books include *A Place to Live: The Crisis of the Cities* (1968), *The Challenge of Megalopolis* (1964), *Life for Dead Spaces* (1963), and *Mid-Century Architecture in America* (1961). He has studied "new towns" here and abroad under a grant from the Ford Foundation, and he is an honorary member of the American Institute of Architects. As architecture critic of the *Washington Post* he writes perceptive and popular articles on architecture, design, and urban problems. His "big picture" orientation toward the city and his interdisciplinary background in communication and architecture made Mr. Von Eckardt an ideal choice to construct an overview of the future of urban communication.

The title of my talk is almost forbidding—"The Future of Communication in Megalopolis." Since I am at a university, I think I should take the proper approach and first define the words in this lengthy title.

FUTURE—I do not really know if the future has a future, particularly today. We talk a lot about the future, and write about it, and publish books about the future, and the science and technology to come, as if it were something entirely different and remote from the past and the present. We do this as if somehow, one day—it is going to be very clean cut — the sun will rise in the West and suddenly we will have a different world.

Well, it is not going to be that way. It will come about very much more gradually. These things we say and write about the future do not take into account that we must apply this technology and science not to what man *does,* but to how man *lives.* And they do not take into account that man does not really change. Nature tends to remain the same and so does man's nature. Taking care of people in their cities is going to mean taking care of the unchanging man and the unchanging demands of Nature. Even though we will be entering the year 2000 soon, we will still need to breathe air and not live under bubbledomes. Mothers will still want to take their babies out into a park. Our demands will be very much the same. Unless we realize that the primary, foremost and, perhaps, only reason for building cities or building an environment is to accommodate the needs of man, all this futurality will fall by the wayside—because it will not meet the needs of man.

In other words, our thinking and our planning about the urban environment cannot be guided only by technocratic possibilities, but they must be guided in terms of human necessities and must be content with the way things basically are. We must become at ease with Nature and with ourselves.

COMMUNICATION—There are many definitions for the word communication. There is communications, plural, which is the technique of communicating—speeches, letters, signals. There is also the dictionary sense: the interchange of thoughts and messages and ideas between people. In essence, that is what civilization is all about.

That is what is breaking down these days. I do not think we can get at the breakdown of communication between generations, between the races, between economic groups, and even now, with the Women's Liberation Movement, between the sexes, by just wondering how we can make better speeches and how we can improve our vocabulary or how we can get at the techniques of communicating. We do need good newspapers, and we ought to do a whole lot more with television than we are doing. But those are matters of technique only. Just improving the techniques of communication is not going to help unless we find the basis of communication. And what *is* the basis of communication? Communication has a great deal to do with community.

Community in America has totally broken down. Not just yesterday and not because of your former governor [Spiro Agnew] here, but over the past 30 or 40 years. It has broken down because we have segregated the American urban environment to an extent that no environment has ever been segregrated before. We are segregated into little communities of people who make $10,000 a year, others of people who make $12,000 a year, and others of people who make below $5,000, etc. We are all over-separated.

How, for instance, can we have community and how can we not have a generation gap if we have a suburban environment in which the children do not have a place to go?

Every time you want to buy a pack of cigarettes or a bar of candy, you have to mobilize 400 horsepower. My children, until they were 14 or 15, had never seen a Negro. I am exaggerating, of course. They had seen maids, but not to talk to, not to play with, not for spontaneous contact. They saw hardly any Jews, and hardly anybody of an income level other than ours. This was in suburbia, but you find the same thing in the city — utter segregation. I am making the point of the total and utter destruction of community in America through urban design, if you will, and planning.

It all came about in the industrial age when the first glue factories smelled and so people did not want a glue factory in their residential area. So we invented the thing called zoning (which is an invitation to bribery and chaos) and tried to keep that glue factory out of the residential district. The profit motive came in, too. It was much easier to sell a house in a neighborhood that was guaranteed to stay at the same or better income level. And there we got into the breaking up of American society—at least in terms of where Americans live—into every sort of sociological, racial and age category.

We even have geriatric ghettos. When you get old enough, we lock you up in Leisure World if you have enough money; if you do not have enough money for Leisure World, we lock you up in what they call housing for the elderly—the Golden Age Clubs, and all that—and you are segregated there. And then we wonder why we cannot get a baby-sitter. The built-in baby-sitter of society that Nature had always provided was Grandma.

You can look at the whole business of community from this angle. With the early homestead anywhere in Western civilization, including the United States, you had not only three or four generations living in the same house, but you also had a great deal of your religious activity and most of your education in the home up to a certain age. It was a place where you got this because that was the center of the farm. From there you got out into the fields and did your threshing and your weeding and whatever.

But then this broke up. The greater specialization

exploded into the village and from there into the city. The more we specialized, the more the community life— the things that bring and hold people together, that hold generations and families together, and, of course, in the larger city, people of various income groups, interests and races — split asunder. And now we are terribly surprised that we do not know how to talk to each other anymore.

But we do not *live* together, we hardly work together, and we hardly know each other. With growing specialization even on the campuses, when was the last time that an architecture student talked to a biology student? The biology lab is two miles away somewhere on the campus. The way campuses are being planned there is no place for the spontaneous get-together. Yes, you can meet at a dance or the Union, but that is a contrived thing where very little happens. Not even the faculty have the spontaneous interdisciplinary meetings anymore because of very bad campus planning. It was actually meant to be segregated that way.

In the "good old days" of the urban crisis, we all talked about, or at least we were made to realize by the blacks in the ghettos, that this society is breaking apart into two societies. The Kerner Commission said so, too.

It is no longer fashionable to talk about it, but that is still very much the case. What has happened since the Kerner Commission Report came out two years ago showing us that we are beginning to have all-black cities surrounded by all-white suburbs—putting a white noose around the black neck—and that this is not going to be a very healthy situation in terms of having a society, having community, and communication? Not a thing has happened except that we have made matters worse. We are still in the same bind.

I think this is the central problem of MEGALOPOLIS, which is the third word in the title of my lecture and which I do not think I need to take much time to define. By megalopolis we simply mean what the British mean by conurbation—that is, particularly along the Eastern Seaboard of the United States but also in the area of the Great Lakes and the West Coast, the cities are sprawling out to such an extent that Los Angeles going meets San Diego coming, and Washington going meets Baltimore coming, and these two are stretching practically to Philadelphia. The whole thing is becoming one urban settlement. This high concentration of urbanization with hardly any distinction between has been called megalopolis—super city. It is used almost entirely as a curse word and a scare word, but actually the high concentration of people, skills, money and talent, etc., is what cities are all about and what civilization is all about. It is not per se a bad thing that a lot of people live on the Eastern Seaboard.

If you look at history and the maps, you will find that people have always congregated along the seaboard, like crabs, and nobody wants to go into the interior where there is nothing. Parenthetically, I think that the notion that is still being bandied about is that it is bad for 75 per cent of the population to live on 3 per cent of the land. But that has always been the case. The highest concentration in the Roman Empire was Rome, and in the Greek civilization it was Athens, and now it is megalopolis. The point is being bandied about that this high concentration along the sea coast and the Great Lakes is bad and, therefore, we have to open up land and build big cities in the middle of nowhere, perhaps somewhere in Minnesota. That is a very intriguing idea. But it will never work.

It is utter nonsense, in my opinion, because (a) there is nothing wrong with megalopolis if you bring order into it and (b) there is never a *raison d'etre* to have a city out in nowhere. Who wants to go there? To what? The reason people come to megalopolis is because the universities are there, the libraries are there, the electronic industry is there and it breeds more electronic industry, and this all builds itself up. It is perfectly possible to make it livable, productive, and nice. And we are *not* running out of land. Just get up in an airplane and look. There is lots of land, but there is bad use of land and a lack of order.

What I really want to address myself to on the future of communication is how to bring about community again, because once you have community again, I think you begin to speak the same language again. To get an understanding of how difficult this is and where to start in even thinking in terms of community, I think we have to take a much more realistic look at what is happening in the inner city, that is, the Negro ghetto. What is happening there is that all of our policies, liberal-conservative, Republican-Democrat, etc., are conspiring to keep people in the ghetto and not let them out. As long as we have that, we are running the danger, as the Kerner Commission pointed out, of two societies, and risking a very, very explosive situation. It is an explosive situation simply because the people are going to get very unhappy and there are going to be more riots. And, the way the climate is being Agnewized and radicalized at the moment, it is not the revolution in the ghetto that I am afraid of. I am afraid of the counter-revolution, which is going to be very rough unless we really start thinking in terms of taking people out of the ghetto.

Bobby Kennedy and other people talked in terms of bringing industry into these Bedford-Stuyvesants so that people can get jobs and being nice to them and improving education there so that they will climb up the ladder of upward mobility and go out and start feeling like white men. After all, they said, the Irish and the Jews and the Poles and the other minority groups have always done it. Well, it is perfectly true that the Jews, the Italians, the Poles, and all the other ethnic groups, when they arrived in this country, had ghettos. These ghettos were pretty horrible. But the Jews, the Irish, and the Poles came at a time when the city was still a manufacturing center, when the city still had small shops, when in the city you still had shoeshine parlors, and you sold newspapers on the street. The little Jewish boy could shine shoes and Papa could work in the garment industry. And Mama probably could also work in the garment industry. Before you knew it, in one generation or so, they could send their son to college. And so they worked their way out of the ghetto.

But what happens when the Negro arrives? His skin keeps him, even if he has money, in the inner city. That is beginning to break down, but that is only a small part of it. The more important part of it is that the restraining of the peasant-type farm worker no longer takes place in the inner city. The industry has left, and no amount of money or black capitalism or exhortations or speeches by Secretary Romney is going to bring industry back into the inner city. You cannot bring in industry of the kind that we need to give a job to the unemployed farm worker from Alabama who has been put out of a job by our farm mechanization and farm subsidies and, therefore, has had to migrate into the city. All he can do, for at least half a generation, if not one generation, is manual semiskilled labor.

But the kind of employment centers—the factories and warehouses—that provide that kind of work are growing and need more space. They do not find that space in the inner city. They need space for their trucks to park, space for adding on to their warehouses, but land in the inner city is fiercely expensive. There is no room to park their trucks, so they move out into Prince George's County and along the lovely Beltway and on Route 128 in Boston and out of Chicago into the suburbs.

The poor Negro who needs that job cannot get out there. Well, why does he not act like a white man and drive a car? Let us just look at the car situation. Twenty-five per cent of the American working wage-earners have no car at all. If you want to know where they are, they are in Watts, and they are in Shaw, and they are in Harlem. And they cannot get out and get the jobs. Some are very brave about the situation and form car pools, and the rest are reduced to riding buses and paying $1.20 and more to get out somewhere to a job. But go out to Fairchild Hiller here in Germantown, Maryland, and see how many buses there are to bring workers in — *none.* There is *no* public transportation. This is also a good part of the Negro ghetto situation that makes them different from the other ethnic groups who climbed the ladder of upward mobility. For the earlier groups, the city was much smaller and they could get around. There was a nickel streetcar and therefore they were not as confined as the Negroes are today. The people in the ghetto now are totally cut off, and this is a vicious circle that *has* to be broken. Why is it a vicious circle? Because the Negro population in the ghettos is multiplying at a faster rate than the rest. The more poor Negroes there are, the more whites move out, and so we are coming to the point of totally white suburbs.

The answer is not having all the blacks in the city—

where they do not have jobs—and all the white middle class in the suburbs—where they do not have jobs—and both of them commuting, passing each other every morning and every night. Without any funds for public transportation, they all have to travel by automobile and so, for instance, about 53 per cent of the District of Columbia land area is given over to automobile, standing or moving, at prices that are up to $100 per square foot. This is insane, absolutely insane. What we need is a planned policy where we decide that this is nonsense.

We have to bring people and their jobs together again. We have to do it through planned communities that are really, truly integrated — not just racially integrated, but economically integrated. People of different income groups should be rubbing elbows, meeting, and to some extent working together. And there you can slowly build up community and communication again, because then people meet in the spare-time activities where there are recreation facilities.

This is happening in some areas. If you have a community where there are Negro children, and Jewish children, and Italian children, and old people and young people, they *are* going to come together. No one has to make any speeches about it, and you do not even have to improve the railroad station or the newspaper, but you are going to have more communication again. *Only* by living together, only by creating an environment and providing facilities in happy surroundings which are conducive to spontaneous human contact can this be done.

The only way we get to a sane and livable environment is by starting with people and bringing people together again. Reston, Virginia, and Columbia, Maryland, are on the road, but it cannot be done by free enterprise alone. If you are trying to do it by really integrating economic and racial groups with meaningful skill, only the government can do it. It can be done—through comprehensive planning done by the federal government and with a real shift in priorities toward building environmental problems. It takes a total commitment, a comprehensive approach which is also largely a physical approach.

The communities of the future, as I see them and as more and more other people do, are not new cities out in nowhere, because new cities are going to be dull as the dickens for the first 30 to 40 years. You also get caught in a terribly vicious circle in just starting them because nobody is going to go out and live in a new city before there is a movie house and a cafe and other things. And how can you have a movie house and cafe if there are no people there? All these attempts to start totally from scratch have been at least terribly slow, and most of them have failed for that reason. You cannot do this thing instantaneously.

But you *can* do it where it really counts in life—which is in the metropolitan area. In other words, you start cleaning up where you have already messed up the place, instead of messing it up out there in Minnesota.

If you start as the Swedes have done with rapid transit and a real interconnection, and if you consider that a new town or community is a satellite to the big city, you will have that natal, real connection between the big city and the towns. So, then, in the beginning, if there is no movie, you can go downtown or to another town where they do have a movie. More important, you have a much greater variety of employment opportunities. If you do not like your job in Reston anymore and there is a fast rapid transit line between it and Columbia, well, you take a job in Columbia. In other words, self-sufficiency, which was the first idea of the new town planners, does not quite work out because our demands are too high. Our ideas of sufficiency have not changed enough. But, fortunately, we can lick that problem with rapid transit and good transportation. This, as a bonus, can reduce the numbers of the automobile, or at least, it can make the automobile a luxury rather than a necessity—and thereby we can reduce the amount of air pollution. This is what I mean by the *comprehensive* approach which can give us not only community, but also, in many other respects, a better environment in which to live.

CHAPTER TEN

Urban Communication: What are the "New Cities" Doing?

by
James W. Rouse
Developer of
Columbia, Maryland

MR. ROUSE is president of The Rouse Company, a mortgage banking and real estate development firm that has created the "new city" of Columbia in the Maryland countryside between Baltimore and Washington. It has been Mr. Rouse's imagination, vision, idealism and integrity that have made Columbia the leading example of the "new town" concept currently being developed in the United States. Columbia has become a mecca, and Mr. Rouse a prophet, for those seeking to know how it can and should be done. He has made a mighty effort at re-establishing community. Among his impressive credits are membership on President Eisenhower's Advisory Committee on Housing, the chairmanship of the subcommittee that recommended the urban renewal program embraced in the Housing Act of 1954, the presidency of Urban America, and a founding role in the Business Committee for the Arts. He has recently been deeply involved in the Department of Housing and Urban Development's efforts to provide large amounts of low-cost housing in America.

I am a long way from being any kind of expert in the area of communication and will not pretend to be one. But I am really happy to extemporize a bit on communication in a very human way because attempting to make communication among the people work is probably one of the most fundamental aspects of the Columbia Plan.

The Columbia Plan is a very important thing to us who are involved in its development. We believe it is the fundamental integrity of the Columbia Plan that has allowed us to win in areas where conventional wisdom would have predicted it was impossible to win—in things such as financing, zoning, education, and dealing with institutions of all kinds.

There has been an extraordinary favorable and supportive reaction to what we are doing by all kinds of political organizations and institutions that do not typically act this way. And we really think that this is because of the fundamental integrity of the Plan itself. We think it makes sense. It is rational. It presents another important alternative for the growth of the metropolitan area, and it answers real problems of growth.

The three fundamental ingredients of the Plan that really interconnect with one another are the public school system, communication, and what we would call "scale" —which can itself be a tool in bringing about effective educational and communication systems or be a result of them.

URBAN COMMUNICATION: WHAT ARE THE "NEW CITIES" DOING?

We started planning Columbia, after we assembled the land, with some specific goals in mind that would motivate and influence the direct planning processes. We held on to those goals and they mattered.

The first goal was to build a real city—a whole city of 100,000 people—in which there would be as many jobs as dwelling units and in which anyone who worked would have the opportunity to live—with housing at rents and prices appropriate to his income. We meant that the full range of activities would be present in education, health, business, industry, libraries, hospitals, restaurants, and concert halls—that the full fabric of the city would be there. This was not a purpose just because we thought it was a good idea. We believed there were some very rational inner relationships among people and the things that people do in the course of life. If our product was to be a city, we needed to account for the things that people do.

Our second goal was to respect the land—the stream valleys, the forests, the slopes, the significant vistas. The land should speak out to control the Plan.

The third and most important goal was to build an environment that would support the growth of people.

The product of a city is not properly measured in brick and mortar, buildings, square feet, rents and prices, but in the total environment that is produced. To be the right kind of product, either in marketable or in public terms, the city should provide an environment that will strengthen the growth of people—of a man and his family.

This was not a sentimental goal, but was based on the belief that if we were really looking at "city" as a product in proper terms and if we dealt with the issues that made a city a good place in which to grow a family, then this would be where people would want to live and businesses would want to locate. Thus we would be dealing with the fundamental motivations that influence the profitability of the product itself. So we found a very precise compatibility between public purpose and private profit in the planning and design and in the development process.

We concluded that we as developers, architects, engineers, and planners — the typical actors in the city-building process — did not have within our own knowledge and experience the capability to design a city if we looked at environment as the product. Therefore, before we ever did any planning or put any lines on paper, we called together a group of 144 people, drawing heavily from the behavioral sciences. The purpose was to bring these people together to engage in conversation in depth with one another and with our staff on what are the optimums in urban life—not educators to talk about education and doctors to talk about health, but everybody to talk about education and health and the other life-support systems. We asked what is the best possible educational system we can conceive of for a city of 100,000 people, and do not worry about whether it is feasible or not—let us see what the optimums are and then be compromised as we go forward. What new things might be possible? How would this influence the physical planning of community?

We wanted to achieve several purposes. We wanted to know how the physical planning process would be influenced by this awareness, how the physical shape of a city enables the birth of institutions and the bringing forth of community in a way that will really be effective in influencing the total environment.

This group met every two or three weeks for two days and a night. We met over a period of about five months, examining questions in education, health, religion, loneliness, delinquency—what works and what does not work in urban society and why.

We had some interesting disciplines for this work group. We said to the group that we did not want a report at the end; we did not care about reaching an agreement. We are the developers, we told them, and we want to engage in this kind of conversation in order to have better light on the work that we have to do. We must make the decisions and cannot shirk the responsibility to do so.

This was a very emancipating set of rules. The fact that no report was going to come out and that nobody had to agree on anything saved months and months of wheel-spinning.

But all of this is a long introduction to the fact that, as we moved forward through this process, it became more and more apparent that the real breakdown in urban life is the breakdown in communication. This inability of people to relate one to another, to relate to groups, to be able to speak under circumstances where they would think they could be heard and where results might occur, we believed to be the most fundamental reason for the basic urban malaise.

There is a sense of aloneness, a sense of the whole thing being bigger than I am and that there is nothing I can do about it. There is a sense of frustration and oppression on the part of little people. But even on the part of the well-to-do there is a sense of being incapable of bringing about results through the existing processes of community. Out of this basic lack of effective communication among people come the conditions that breed the hostility and fear and separation and division and conflict. There is this inability of people to change their institutions because they cannot get at the institutions with other people who think as they do because they cannot find those people. People of like-mindedness do not have the opportunity to find themselves in natural association. The fundamental ingredients of community, looked at in human terms, simply do not exist in urban society today, and they do not exist any more in the suburbs than in the ghetto — if as much. In the massiveness of the city there is little or no physical definition of community—no arrangement of community institutions such as schools, churches, or health centers that bring people together in relationship with one another. There is an irrational scattering of the institutions and natural meeting places and an absence of any physically defined community, with the result that people live in a kind of negative, impersonal, depersonalized massiveness.

When you move out into the suburbs it becomes worse—with houses on individual lots spacing fewer people over larger areas, no rational relationship between school, church, or any of the activities in which people are engaged. A child in the suburb has no chance to find other children except in a very limited sense, and no opportunity to make choices about going fishing, or to a music lesson, the library or a concert without someone taking him there in an automobile. He even lacks the choice of public transportation. Therefore, as we examined the Columbia prospect, we became convinced that the fundamental discipline of the Plan had to be to magnify every opportunity to create a physical sense of community in order that there could be a human sense of community—in order then that people would come together in a natural, unself-conscious way day-by-day under circumstances where they would know one another, come to trust one another, and be able to share hopes, fears, and frustrations with the ability to do something about them.

Thus, the first element in the hierarchy of communities was the neighborhoood. The control on the size of the neighborhood became the elementary school, which seemed to us to be the first integrating community force in urban life. We plumped for small schools instead of big schools. We were trying to hold them to 500 to 600 students. This meant about 1,200 families in a place where we would have to put all the other things. With the school we put the other services for that kind of population—a child care center, swimming pool, park, playground, meeting room, and small store—a restoration of the old corner drugstore-grocer concept at the heart of the neighborhood. This meant also a path system to connect the people in the neighborhood to the central place so that a mother with children of baby-carriage age could go someplace with the prospect that other people would be there—in the meeting room, or the child care center, or school, store, or snack bar. Meeting would become a function of the neighborhood, meetings that would not occur if all these things were scattered across the landscape and were reached only by automobile.

Three or four of these neighborhoods constitute a village — which means a population of 12,000 to 15,000 people. We got there by examining the basic life systems of high schools, middle schools, churches, health, and medical centers. We found that there was an extraordinary overlay of optimum markets—that a population of 10,000 to 15,000 people would support a high school of about 1,200 students, a middle school with three grades of about 900 students, a supermarket, a medical center, a variety of churches and a library.

One by one, these functions of life began to be served, we believed in optimum terms in this kind of population. And, therefore, this became the village center where high school, middle school, churches, basic community meeting rooms, supermarket, medical center, and library would all be in one place. And, as a result of being in one place, there would again be the kind of natural unself-conscious meeting of teacher, student, minister, parent, merchant, doctor—in the normal course of life, in a population size in which people were capable of knowing a great many other people and, therefore, feeling comfortable, secure, and willing to communicate with one another, more able to do something about whatever it was that needed to be done.

The third element in the hierarchy of the Plan was downtown—where we tried to concentrate the major institutional life of the community — the one-of-a-kind services and major businesses—department stores, specialty shops, office buildings, theaters, restaurants, hotels, major entertainment, cultural and recreational facilities, and colleges.

Important to the communication system is a transportation system that gives the people the opportunity to move—which connects all the village centers with one another and with downtown and major places of employment.

It is much too early to make any final, definitive judgments about Columbia. But there are some things that we feel very good about, and one is this basic system of scale, of neighborhoods and villages that are visible, separated from one another by open space — by forests and streams. You know where a neighborhood or village begins and ends. There is a real sense of being in a physical community at these levels. Another is the fact that there has been an extraordinary, spontaneous burst of activity on the part of people in forming organizations of all kinds, serving all sorts of special interests. Columbia has only 7,000 people today, but if you took any other suburban population of 7,000 in the Baltimore-Washington region and compared it with Columbia, you would see no such quality of expression on the part of the people — of getting together and taking action on things important to them.

We have learned that this product—a good environment — has all the appeal and meaning we hoped it would. Business and industry have been attracted by the fact that Columbia is an appealing place for their workers to live. We started out estimating that we would have 30,000 jobs and 30,000 dwelling units, but now it looks like 60,000 jobs and 30,000 dwelling units. A new school system has been set up in a conservative county by a conservative school board. The schools in Columbia are ungraded, have open classrooms, team teaching, no marks, narrative reports, and focus on the development of the individual child.

The churches have responded to the opportunity brought about by the integrity of the Plan — 15 Protestant denominations, the Catholic church, and the Jews together creating a Religious Facilities Corporation that owns all the church buildings. They will share space, staff, and program.

The Johns Hopkins Medical Institutions have brought in a voluntary, comprehensive health care plan — any family in Columbia with four or more people, whatever the number, can, for $43.50 a month, have comprehensive health care including home nursing service, group medical practice, hospitalization, and psychiatric care—all provided by the Johns Hopkins Medical Institutions. These things come out of the basic integrity of the Plan.

All this has provided experience that is now being drawn into an effort to feed back into the life of an old city. We are working under a contract with the business community of Hartford, Connecticut, to set up in the next two years a process to make the entire Hartford region work the way a region ought to work. This means exploring simultaneously all the processes of education, health, communication, law and justice, welfare, housing, and employment.

Assuming that we can do what we know how to do in America, assuming that we can do it all at the same time, and assuming that—if we did do it all at the same time—the trade-offs that could occur in making systems work would make it possible to bring about the best kind of educational system and health system and law and justice, etc., this then could constitute the beginning of all planning and we could build from this process physical models of new communities throughout the Hartford region — schedule it; program it; organize for it; test out the arithmetic for it; and prove that it *is* possible to make an existing metropolitan region work.

In undertaking this study, one of the first things that we did was to interview three hundred persons throughout the Hartford region, through as wide a spectrum as we could cover. We were asking three questions: "What is life like in Hartford? What do you think it might be? What is keeeping it from being that?"

The answers to the first two questions varied enormously. But it did not matter to whom we were talking, the answer to the third question was the same from almost anyone, from the ghetto to the suburbs: "I can't do anything about it. There's no way of influencing the result." This sense of separation, of powerlessness, is a prevailing mood. It is not just a ghetto mood. It is a prevailing mood in urban society.

This is a problem in communication. One of the things that our examination of life in the region of Hartford, an old city, told us is that it is absolutely essential to making a city work that we create physical and institutional circumstances in which there is an opportunity for people to relate to one another and to their institutions. They should be a part of them, be able to modify them, throw them out, start them over, and feel that the physical and institutional community is theirs, not that they live as human beings oppressed by and separated from or denied life by the civilization of which they are a part.

We think that this can happen. You *can* reorganize a school system. You *can* create a comprehensive health care system. You *can* break down and create whole new systems of law and justice so that the guy who represents security to the people of a neighborhood could be a distinguished guy in that neighborhood who wears a red jacket and a whistle instead of a cap and a revolver and a nightstick. A sense of community can be created both physically and institutionally and, under these circumstances, people will communicate. And then, if people do communicate under circumstances where they think they can be heard and where something may happen, the city begins to work again.

Until we accomplish this, we are just playing games. All of the business about housing, employment, job training, and the poverty programs is putting bandages on open wounds, but it does not have anything to do with curing the problems of the city. Urban renewal as it is now conducted, and the poverty program as it is now and has been conducted, have produced no substantial relief in the quality of life in the city. I think that the most optimistic view of the quality of urban life would have to say that it has gone steadily downhill over the last 30 years despite larger and larger programs that we have mounted to deal with it because we keep dealing with the symptoms—with the gaps, with the products of non-community and non-communication. We have got to get back to the roots of these conditions and then work out into physical plans and into housing and into job training. All of these things have to happen, but they have to happen as a process of making life work — not just dealing with the symptoms of life not working.

The fear-hostility syndrome is the most paralyzing aspect of American life today—wherever it is—and it is everywhere. It is not just an inner-city condition. Let somebody go out into a suburb and try to build a low-rent housing project and everybody is up in arms because they are terrified — they do not know what is going to happen— and then comes the hostility and the conflict and the battle. This would have happened to us in Howard County. But now we are having pressure put on us in Columbia by the government and the people in Howard County that we are not building *enough* low-income housing. This would never have been possible in a subdivision. It is only in the context of a city that it is possible. And here we came along in 1963 to build a city in Howard County. What we had to deal with in prospect was the same fear-hostility conflict. Everybody was scared to death because we were talking about building townhouses and highrise apartments and shopping centers and factories and all the bad things of a city—what they wanted was a bucolic county.

And yet we were able, in presenting a plan that rationally dealt with the real problem of growth — such real problems as where the money is coming from to pay for the schools to provide for the expanding population —to show that we had a much greater prospect of producing that business and industry that could pay for schools in a rational city, and that we would be able to deal one by one with the real problems that the county faces. And in 1965, when we went in to have a public zoning hearing in that kind of county under those circumstances, not one single person in Howard County appeared to oppose the zoning. This was an incredible thing. This was really an experience in communication. And it was not selling. We had no political strength. We had no power on our side at all. But we were dealing with the real conditions of the county and we were proposing real solutions and we were communicating them. I am certain that if we had come along and applied for zoning back when we decided to build a city and *then* set about the planning and *then* set about selling it, it never would have won in a thousand years, because we would have stimulated fears that we never could have harnessed after that.

Edmund M. Midura, an assistant professor in the Department of Journalism at the University of Maryland, was chairman of the *Baltimore Sun* Distinguished Lectures Series in 1970. He is a former newspaperman with the *Milwaukee Journal*, the *Utica Daily Press*, and others. He has taught at the Universities of Maryland, Iowa and Rhode Island and at the Pennsylvania State University. He received his doctorate in mass communication from the University of Iowa and his other degrees from Utica College of Syracuse University and the Pennsylvania State University.

Index

Index

A

AFL-CIO 145
Agnew, Spiro T. 67, 71, 81, 143, 156, 161
Albany, N.Y. 11
Altadena, Calif. 130
American Broadcasting Co. 79
American Dental Association 68-69
Anacostia 74
Anti-war moratorium, Washington 64-66
Athens 160

B

Baltimore 8, 74, 80, 159
Baltimore *Evening Sun* 34
Banfield, Edward 83
"The Battle of East St. Louis" 78
Bayh, Birch 145
Bedford-Stuyvesant 161
Before the Mayflower 94
Bennett, Lerone 94
Beverly Hills High School 128
Black communicators, role of 96-97
Black Muslims 38
Black Panthers 38, 75, 81, 96
Boston 163
Brinkley, David 67
Brown, Claude 121

C

Caldwell, Earl 96-97
Cambodia 81
Carmichael, Stokeley 72
Carroll, Diahann 70
Carswell, G. Harrold 145
"Charcoal Alley No. 1" 128
Chew, Birdell 124-126
Chicago 163
Chisholm, Shirley 83
Citizens Communication Center 111
Clark, Jim 72
Clark, Kenneth 120
Cleveland 8, 16
Columbia Broadcasting System 78
Columbia Journalism Review 74
Columbia, Md. 165, 166, 170-179, 182-183
Columbia (Md.) Plan 170-179
Columbia (Md.) Religious Facilities Corp. 179

Committee on Racial Equality 38, 50
Communications Act of 1934 109
Community Coalition on Broadcasting 111
"Community" concept 155-156, 164-165, 174-177, 178
Congress, U. S. 103, 109, 129-130
Connor, Bull 72
Crest toothpaste 68

D

Detroit, 8, 51
"Direct Line" 40-41
Douglass, Frederick 127
Douglass House 127

E

Eagles Club 50
East Cleveland, Ohio 16
Eastern Seaboard 159-160
East Los Angeles, Calif. 130
East St. Louis, Ill. 78, 79, 80
Ebony 92-94
Emergency Committee on the Transportation Crisis 140
Evans, Emmery 125
"The Eye of the Storm" 79

F

Fairchild-Hiller Corp. 163
Fairness Doctrine 110
Federal Communications Commission 65, 76-77, 108-112
From the Ashes 125

G

Gallup, George 75
Great Lakes 159-160
Greece 66, 160
Greenberg, Bradley S. 9; biography, 15; 16-28
Groppi, James 45-46, 48-51, 55-58

H

Hanson, Royce 12; biography, 135; 136-149
Harlem 70, 74, 163
Harris, Sammy 122-124, 127
Hartford, Conn. 179-181
Heisler, Philip S. 10; biography, 31; 32-42
Holman, Benjamin F. 10; biography, 101; 102-112
Honolulu 59
Howard County, Md. 182-183

I

Infinite 122-123

J

Jackson, James Thomas 124
Johns Hopkins Medical Institutions 179
Johnson, John H. 10; biography, 89; 90-97
Johnson, Lyndon B. 74
Jordan Downs 117
"Julia" 70
Justice Dept. Community Relations Service 102-107, 112

K

Kennedy, John F., quotation, 6; 74
Kennedy, Robert 161
Kennedy, Vallejo Ryan 125
Kerner Commission quotations, 6; 16; quotations, 36; 93, 106-107, 112, 158-159, 161
Kerner Report 106-107, 112, 158-159, 161
King, Martin Luther, Jr. 72, 79
Klein, "Woody" 10-12
KTAL-TV 111

L

Lansing, Mich. 16
Lindsay, John V. 10-12
Lippmann, Walter 138, 145
Long Beach, Calif. 130
Los Angeles 8, 59, 116, 159
Los Angeles 128

M

Madison, Wis. 46
Maier, Henry 56-59
Malcolm X 120
Man Child in the Promised Land 120
McLuhan, Marshall 107-108, 142
Media use, adults' 23-28
Media use, childrens' 17-23
Media use, Negroes' 35, 53-54
Milwaukee 8, 45-46, 48-53, 55-58
"Milwaukee 14" 46
Milwaukee *Journal* 48-59
Minneapolis 59
Model Cities program 46, 58
"Mod Squad" 70

Monroe, William, Jr. 10; biography, 63; 64-85
Moynihan, Daniel Patrick 74
Moynihan Report 96
My Bondage and My Freedom 127

N

National Advisory Commission on Civil Disorders (Kerner Commission) quotations, 6; 16; quotations, 36; 93, 106-107, 112, 158-159, 161
National Association for the Advancement of Colored People 38, 50, 75, 119
National Broadcasting Co. 65, 67, 127
Newark, N.J. 8, 51
New Orleans 71
News coverage, inner city 34-42
News coverage of extremists 104
News coverage of minority groups 106
News coverage of rioting 52-53, 56-57
News coverage, suburban 33
News, television 22-23, 24, 26-27, 65-83
New York City 10-12
New York *Times* 76, 96, 121
Nixon, Pat 65
Nixon, Richard M. 65, 81
Nixon, Tricia 65
Northwestern University 37

O

Office of Economic Opportunity 25
One, Two, Three 123
One Year Later 107

P

Pasadena, Calif. 130
Philadelphia 16, 21, 159
Philadelphia *Bulletin* 74
Philadelphia Plan 81
Powell, Adam Clayton, Jr. 80
Prejudice Anonymous 80
Primer of Ascertainment of Community Problems 108-109
Prince George's County, Md. 163

R

Rauh, Joseph 145
Reston, Va. 165, 166
Ribicoff, Abraham 129-130
Riceville, Iowa 79, 80
Rochester, N.Y. 8
Roman Empire 160
Romney, George 162
Rouse, James W. 12; biography, 169; 170-183
Russia 66

S

San Bernardino, Calif. 130
San Deigo, Calif. 159
San Francisco 96, 130
Scholastic 128
Schulberg, Budd 12; biography, 115; 116-131
Schulberg, Stuart 81
Scott, Johnie 127
Shaw 163
Shaw, George Bernard, quotation, 90
Shoquist, Joseph W. 10; biography, 45; 46-60
Stone, Chuck 80-81
Supreme Court, U.S. 145-147

T

Television, role of 65-83
Texarkana, Ark. 111
"Today" 81
"Triple O" 58
TV Guide 70

U

The Unheavenly City 83
United Church of Christ 110, 111
Urban Coalition 106-107
Urban Journalism Center 37
Urban League 38, 75

V

Viet Nam 73, 74, 81
Vinson, Fred 146-147
VISTA 37
Von Eckardt, Wolf 12; biography, 153; 154-166

W

Wallace, George C. 74
Washington, D.C. 8, 11, 64-65, 83, 103, 140, 159, 164
Watts 51, 116-120, 127, 130-131, 163
Watts Summer Festival 126
Watts Writers Workshop 127-130
Wauwatosa, Wis. 51
Westminster 117-118
The White Problem in America 93
Wilkins, Roy 145
Williams, Clarence 70
WLBT-TV 110
WNEW 82
Women's Liberation Movement 155
World War II 32-33

RENEWALS 691-4574
DATE DUE